NEW
YORK

NEW
ENGLAND

P ROYAL

LVANIA

Charles T

PLYMOUTH

BOSTON

THE

NORTHERN OCEAN

OR SEA

N YORK

arles Town

LURELLE

The
Geography
of
American Antiques

Frederick W. Whitney

1929

TREASURE TROVE

From the Painting by Lurelle Guild

The
Geography
of
American Antiques

Text and Illustrations

by

Lurelle Van Arsdale Guild

GARDEN CITY   1929   NEW YORK

DOUBLEDAY, DORAN AND COMPANY, INC.

DEDICATED
TO
MY MOTHER

ACKNOWLEDGMENT

In the compiling of this book I have been forced to depend upon private collectors and museums for aid in assembling suitable material. In every case my requests met with generous coöperation, and I wish to take this opportunity of thanking collectively, and in thought individually, those who have helped me make this book an actuality.

L. V. A. G.

FOREWORD

THE printed word allows me to describe for you shapes and forms of furniture but it can in no way paint in your mind the feeling and texture of old woods. This sensitiveness can be acquired only through years of practical experience and intensely interested study. I shall keep within these limitations and my aim shall be rather to show the varied influences which left their marks on the construction and embellishments of the furniture of our forefathers.

An exhaustive study of the great social and political forces which deeply affect a nation must be made before one can really attempt to understand the changes which take place in the furniture of that nation; for each country reflects with precision in her furniture craft the sentiments, aspirations, and intellectual ability of her people as well as their racial derivation and the type of life which they lead. And so, in an amazing fashion, we can trace the decrees of a strong government, the prohibitive measures of a despotic one, wars, and internal strife, etched deeply though unconsciously upon the character and turnings of furniture. The history of a period style is in itself an almost comprehensive history of the nation which produced it, so inexorably bound are they.

Bearing this in mind, we can readily see that New England, a strong British colony, would produce a completely different type of furniture than Pennsylvania, where from the start we find a strong German-Dutch predominance. And so, too, when we consider that prior to 1790 nine nations played noteworthy parts in the colonizing of the Atlantic seaboard, we can more easily understand the vast difference which we meet in furniture specimens from the various colonies.

I hope to show in this volume how these varied racial influences were absorbed and fused until in some cases we find them completely obliterated and in others replaced with a new sort of expression retaining much of the old but embellishing it with that which is distinctly the product of the new life.

Dissension between the mother countries of these provinces, mutual hardships and sufferings, mutual problems and solutions in this strange new land slowly but firmly established an unbreakable bond between them. In the course of time, England gained control of nearly all the seaboard colonies, and by the tyrannical measures which she imposed unknowingly cemented that unity which led them to take their stand together to oppose her as a common enemy and which later resulted in the casting aside forever of their petty prejudices and differences, and the formation of a new nation.

While this political unification had been taking place a similar movement was felt in the mobiliary arts. An enforced unity of thought had left its effects upon furniture, and after the close of the Revolution we find that each year it grows more difficult to trace the differences in the furniture craft of the various states.

Naturally the feeling produced by the war cut off nearly all our trade with that nation upon whom prior to the war we had depended for many of the necessities as well as the few luxuries which the times permitted. A large amount of this trade we know went to France, but the awakening of national consciousness and the responsibility of building up the country's enterprises and putting her on an acknowledgedly good financial basis called for American-made products wherever possible and we find home industry being sponsored by such men as Savery, Goddard, and later Hitchcock and Duncan Phyfe.

There has always been much controversy over America's laxity and tardiness in producing a great period furniture. The complaint is that we are still borrowing, and inexcusably, from European countries. Let us be generous enough to realize that more than three hundred years will be necessary to fuse the various elements which have made our nation and from which she still is drawing. To our generation falls the task of building a background against which coming generations may create. Neither France nor England produced a distinct style that was noteworthy in the first 300 years of their national existence, yet in the bloom which followed these periods of establishment, they gave the world their most famous and most beautiful styles. Perhaps America's contribution to the history of furniture will be next.

CONTENTS

INTRODUCTION

IN undertaking a study of the early furniture produced in this country we must, of necessity, give our first consideration to the peoples who colonized the land; the racial influences which they brought from their mother countries, the type of life they were forced by climate and isolation to lead, and lastly their character as influenced through generations by religion, political affiliation, poverty, wealth, and station in life.

Some consideration must also be given to conditions in Europe during the early part of the Seventeenth Century before we can appreciate the motives which lay behind American colonization.

Instability of the reigning houses in France and England, religious unrest throughout the entire continent, marked decline in the power of Spain and Portugal, with ensuing wars, were all no doubt directly the results of the Renaissance and the new thinking which was sweeping clean the entire civilized world. And through turbulences, wars, and the downfall of ancient dynasties and civilizations were being laid the foundations of modern commercial, economic, and political history.

The Sixteenth Century had witnessed attempts to colonize America but in almost every case with no permanent results. To be certain, Mexico had been conquered by Cortez, in 1519, and St. Augustine was founded in 1564 by a colony of Huguenots, but neither of these events played much of a part in American history prior to the Revolution. We are much more interested in Raleigh's unsuccessful colony at Roanoke and other lost colonies throughout Maine and Rhode Island.

On a Friday night December 21, 1620, the third exploring party from the *Mayflower* landed at Plymouth after having searched the coast for two months for a favorable spot on which to settle. The following day the *Mayflower* was signaled and the choice declared to those who had remained aboard. Seventy-three men and twenty-nine women constituted this brave little band facing a desolate winter in a strange, barbaric country inhabited by an unknown savage race. Aboard the vessel fever was taking its toll and living conditions were far from satisfactory. The first problem which the men of the group faced was to provide shelter for the women and the sick.

It is most regrettable that of these early homes we have little in the way of authentic description. From the few records of the times we can gather that the men lived ashore in wigwams while the buildings were in construction, with intermittent trips to the *Mayflower*, lying in the harbor. We know, too, that the dire need for shelter prevented them from spending much time on style and finish in the homes which they erected. Rough-hewn logs sufficed because lack of time and tools prevented their planing. Thatch or log roofs were used and no doubt clay chimneys, though we may safely suppose that many of the chimneys were also constructed of logs because of the innumerable fires which ravished the homes of the settlement from 1620 to 1630.

With our knowledge of the humbleness of these first buildings, the lack of tools and expert builders, we may truly marvel at those which we know existed fifteen years later. Homes that warranted more than passing attention from European travelers in the colonies; mansions built in contemporary English style and rivaling the best of England's own; pretentious pieces of architecture furnished with local though more often imported fabrics and furniture. And the appalling fact behind this unprecedented building was that such homes were not uncommon throughout New England.

In searching for the motive behind this growth we may justly credit much of it to the fact that almost daily after 1625 new groups of friends and relatives were arriving bringing with them good cheer and news and keeping fresh in the hearts of the colonists the memories of dear old Eng-land. Much, too, must be attributed to the native thrift of the men and women who made this colony; whose love of the life which they left behind them in England moved them to reëstablish it to the best of their ability over here; and lastly to the establishment of a normal social life.

After the first homes had been erected, attention was turned to the few pieces of furniture necessary to make them livable. And few they were those first two winters, for time was filled wresting a living from the land and forests and protecting the little settlement from the Indians. The orig-inal band from the *Mayflower* was daily being diminished by sickness and misfortune, and the vital problem of keeping as many as possible alive kept the more rugged busy and occupied time that might have, under more normal circumstances, been spent perfecting and embellishing the home.

We can scarcely suppose that the Pilgrim Fathers, buffeted by perse-cutions, sickness, and death, carried to this new land by their staunch and rugged spirits, indomitable courage, and sense of justice could have, when necessity demanded, produced aught else than the sturdy stout furniture which we know to-day as their handicraft. Somber and even crude, it per-sonifies the coarse manners and dogmatic firmness of the men who made it, and aside from the personal sentiment which we may feel in regard to it we must recognize the value, from a purely historical point of view, gained from the study of it.

We can find no record of an experienced cabinetworker aboard the *Mayflower* on either of her first two trips, although we do know that John Alden was credited with some experience as a joiner and that in 1623 the *Charity* brought to Plymouth a shipbuilder, who may or may not have turned a hand to cabinetwork. Even so, one or two men could not have made the furniture for the whole group and we must consider it as the work of men without training, hampered no doubt by a lack of tools but with an inherent knowledge of the furniture of their native land. So they created what we to-day call Pilgrim furniture, reminiscent without doubt of the land of their birth but withal different. A new furniture, a new expression, of men produced by a highly developed civilization and transposed through trials, grief, and disaster to a wild, an unknown land, and there even as the savage forced to work out their own salvation with and by means of whatever their ingenuity could devise.

Here let us note that when the Pilgrims left England in 1620 the Jacobean element was still in prominence, and nearly all the furniture of that period was constructed of oak. This will explain the natural tendency of the men at Plymouth to seek oak for the first pieces which they made. Later, when more familiar with their problems, we find them supplanting oak with pine, because it was abundant throughout the near-by forests and easier to obtain and because its grain and softness were better suited to their purpose.

So much for Massachusetts, the epitome of American Independence. Let us now consider and contrast another and contemporary British colony, Virginia. In speaking of the early settlers of Massachusetts, we have termed them a group, fleeing religious persecution and taxation and seeking a spot where they might worship their God in the manner which they chose. To be certain, there were other elements amongst them, but the character of the group was established by such men as Winslow, Bradford, Standish, Alden, and others, whom we find in predominant numbers. Men from humble and even poverty-stricken homes, graced with a steadfastness of purpose and conviction which political upheavals could not shake nor alter; blessed with a tranquillity of mind that unmoved by opposition and hardship sought no more than peace and freedom.

In strong contrast are the earliest settlers of Virginia. Here we encounter a band of fifty or sixty gentlemen adventurers accompanied by as many more servants and laborers. Hangers-on of the court, noblemen, and favorites of a weak king. Virile men of an age of exploration, seeking adventure and conquest for their country and caring little what sacrifices might be asked of them in gaining their goal. It is far from my mind to degradate the names of the Virginia colonists. They gladly went forth to face untold deaths and did it with a gesture and a swagger that well bespoke their adventuresome spirits and which wrote pages of romance into the history of America. If their object in colonizing differed from the New England settlers, we can find little difference in the sufferings which they endured here. Few indeed of them lived to return to that country whose glories they had embellished.

I wish merely to show by the comparison which I have drawn how two groups of men born of the same race but with totally different backgrounds when placed under similar conditions will express themselves in a very different manner when necessity forces them through the medium of the household crafts.

Pennsylvania we find a prosperous colony from the start. Under the military jurisdiction of the Dutch East India Company, from 1604 to 1664, practically no settlements were attempted aside from a small Swedish colony at Chester. In 1681, Charles II granted the region west of the Delaware to William Penn, the Quaker, and in 1682 the "city of brotherly love" was founded. Strange, indeed, were this peaceful, industrious colony and the principles upon which it was builded. The strong personality of generous, peace-loving Penn pervaded the whole settlement. Swedes coalesced readily with the Quakers, and generous treaties with the Indians made of them lifelong friends.

Between 1715 and 1735 additional bodies of immigrants, Scotch-Irish and German, joined the colony. Penn's government remained in force until Pennsylvania joined the other colonies in the fight for freedom.

Seemingly the wisdom, foresight, and gentleness of William Penn in his dealings with both settlers and Indians eradicated in the history of this colony the strife and Indian wars which so often hazarded the welfare and retarded the development of the other settlements.

And so, we can go through every colony and find each expressing unknowingly her ability or inability to adjust herself to the new life. But much of this is evident at a glance and we may leave it here and touch upon it later when specific detail demands.

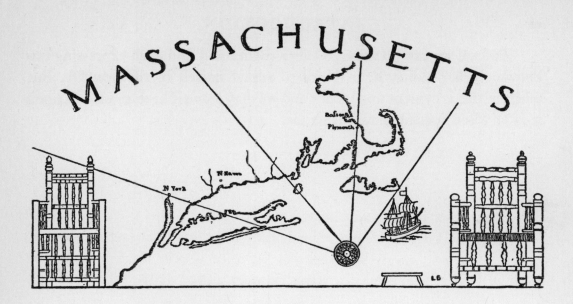

The Geography of
American Antiques

CHAPTER I

PILGRIM FURNITURE

A STUDY of the household arts of any nation in any age will show that a position of primary importance has always been given to the chest, and that many other pieces of furniture have been mere outgrowths or developments of it. It is probable that this came about because of the many services which a box or chest may render; it may be container, table, and seat in one.

This development is readily traced in New England, for the early colonist had more use for a chest into which he might pack his belongings and flee when Indian raids and other dire disasters threatened than he had for a table from which to eat or a chair upon which to sit. Records show that in 1626 there were several "joiners, carpenters, and sawiers" in the colony, but labor was high and the majority of homes still depended for furnishings on the skilled hand of the master of the house. Chairs ranked among the expensive pieces, and wills and inventories of the time show two or possibly three of them numbered in a man's goods compared to eighteen to twenty-five "formes" or benches.

Let us go back to England before the Pilgrims set sail. Toward the end of the Fifteenth Century, practically every household equipment need was served by a simple chest in which the sides extended lower than the front and the back to form feet and keep the body of the chest off the floor. The members were held together by crude iron or leather straps, or oak dowels, and sometimes by hand-wrought nails (a note for those who believe the nail a modern invention). These chests were almost invariably constructed of oak throughout and a crude wire run through rough holes in the back and lid served as a hinge when the strap hinge was not employed. Up to the middle of the Seventeenth Century the wood used was about three quarters of an inch thick. The locks were of hand-wrought iron and marked with the same workmanship which we find on the hinges. A hinge staple fastened on the inside of the lid in the center front fitted into a hole in the lock front when closed. The paneled walls which were so popular throughout the Elizabethan and Jacobean periods left a strong influence on the chest, and nearly all the better-known styles of paneling may be found in one way or another used on this article of furniture.

When the first chest was made in this country it is only logical to suppose that it was

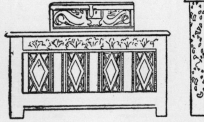 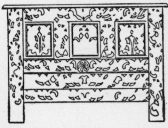 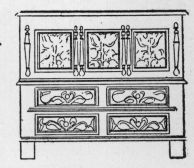

DEVELOPMENT FROM BIBLE-BOX TO HIGHBOY

fashioned after the traditions of the English and the methods followed were those which had been employed in the mother country.

Solidity of construction was a primary aim in all the early furniture and we find the colonist, with this in view, discarding any use of glue and substituting wooden pegs to hold together the various parts. Joints connecting rails and stiles were mortised and tenoned and held securely by square dowel pegs driven completely through round holes. The even or flush surfaces of all the outer faces, as well as the junction of the stiles with the rails and the underframing with the legs, were a prominent characteristic of the oak-framed chest. This was done to secure sound construction in the framing, for the pegs were placed very close to the mortised members and the driving of the pegs would have caused the wood to split had not the shoulder of the tenon been flush and tight to the edge to prevent this. We find this detail retained in late Eighteenth Century mahogany furniture.

Many English chests had paneled lids, a feature which rarely appears in an American chest, and in the latter, though the body construction may be of oak, we are apt to discover a pine lid; we can imagine the colonist weakening a bit after the chest proper had been made and finishing it

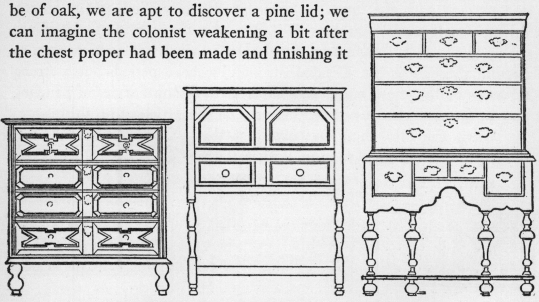

DEVELOPMENT FROM BIBLE-BOX TO HIGHBOY

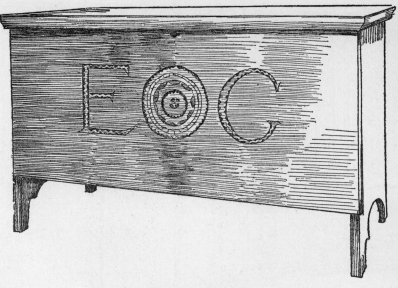

EARLY CARVED
SIX-BOARD PINE CHEST

off with a lid of a single piece of pine, which was so easy to work. For this reason, too, we often find the lid missing, probably because the wire hinges had pulled through the soft wood or the wood itself had worn down sufficiently to cause it to be discarded or replaced. It is also characteristic of the American carved or paneled chest to find the feet formed by a continuation of the stiles on both the front and the back.

How many times upon raising the lid we have found little box compartments at one end of the chest, constructed simply of three pieces of wood with a common swinging lid. Sometimes we may observe that to avoid nailing they were held in place by grooves. These boxes served to hold small trinkets and family papers that might become lost in the depths of the chest.

The idea of making his product more time-saving, or perhaps more convenient, led the cabinetmaker and joiner to elaborate the chest to the point of adding a drawer in the lower part. One can readily imagine the

OAK CHEST SHOWING ARCHITECTURAL DETAILS

asset it would be, for now it was possible to make an assortment of contents, and the most-needed articles could be placed in the drawer, thereby eliminating a search through the entire chest to reach the bottom. This drawer may also have held the various articles which were wont to clutter the top and which had to be removed before the lid could be raised. The larger drawer we sometimes find replaced by two smaller drawers placed side by side. Still greater elaboration appears in the Hadley chest, and sometimes we find two and three drawers, one above the other. To be sure, by 1760 the newer arrivals from England had brought many chests that boasted three and even four drawers, and were decorated with corbels and applied moldings, in the fashion of court cupboards. Made of oak, they seemed to reflect the architecture of England, and we cannot deny their beauty, for they showed exquisite workmanship; nevertheless, there lies a charm in the irregularity or perhaps uncertainty of craftsmanship which

ONE-DRAWER LINEN CHEST

the colonial worker put into his efforts and his products, and even when these cannot compare in workmanship with the imported articles, they are equally pleasant in appearance.

Practicability creeps in again and the chest is put upon a frame, a change inspired perhaps by a joiner's placing a chest on a stretcher table while working upon it or possibly by the housewife who found it unpleasant to be forced to lean over the low chest every time she wanted to get something out of it. One might imagine

CARVED HADLEY CHEST

that they were bulky, considering their exterior height of about thirty-six inches and interior depth of about eighteen, but they were practical enough to warrant their construction.

The legs of the frame were usually turned, with flat or turned stretchers running into a block at the base of the leg. The leg met squarely with the underframing of the chest

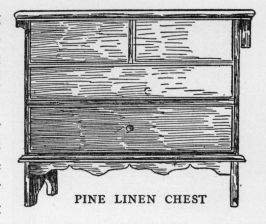

PINE LINEN CHEST

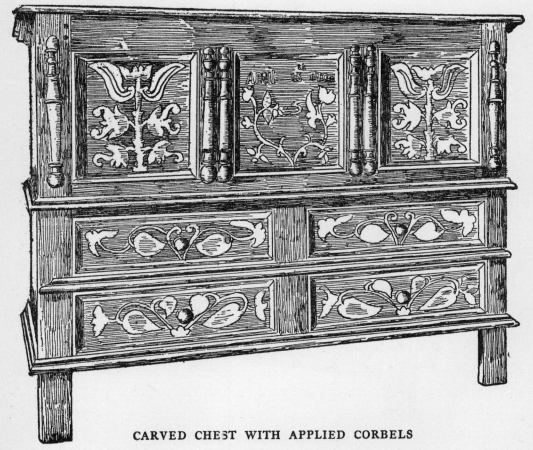

CARVED CHEST WITH APPLIED CORBELS

CONNECTICUT CHEST
OF OAK

LINEN CHEST OF PINE WITH
SCROLL FEET

BALL-FOOT LINEN CHEST

and extended in a rectangular block to the lid to form the side construction. Practically every chest of this type had a drawer, either paneled or carved.

HEAVY OAK BALL-FOOT CHEST WITH APPLIED MOLDING

We can readily believe that the colonists would do a certain amount of ecclesiastical carving on these early pieces and with it purely architectural embellishments, as well as scratch carving, the latter offering a quick and effective means of relieving a plain surface. The dignified and beautiful carving of Gothic origin was well adapted to the oak chest, for the perpendicular line of Gothic tracery could follow the grain of the wood where a more delicate and complex pattern would have been nearly impossible because of the hardness of the wood. Pine was more readily worked.

PAINTED LINEN CHEST OF PINE

It was only the wealthy man of the time who could order his crafts-man to produce a chest for his particular need and decorated to suit his own peculiar fancy, but these chests remain, nevertheless, one of the most interesting phases in the study of antique furniture. The less fortunate soul, no doubt wishing to have something equally beautiful as his neighbor's and not completely satisfied with a mere box of six boards to grace his humble home, selected pine or whitewood (the latter more graciously called tulip wood) with which to work. As paneling, as well as scratch carving

EARLY OAK BIBLE-BOX

DESK-ON-A-FRAME OF MAPLE AND PINE

of the better sort, was a time-taking task, he employed his native ingenuity and painted the chest in shades of Indian red, blue, and yellow. This

BIBLE-BOX OF PINE AND OAK

type of chest has always caught my fancy, for it shows the first true painted decoration in this country, and many representatives of this type show as well true evidence of artistic ability. Sometimes we find one

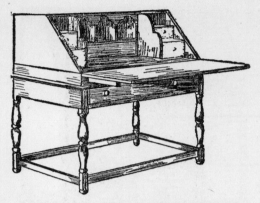

DESK-ON-A-FRAME WITH PULLS

or two drawers, each having a different motif without breaking the effect of the pattern as a whole.

While considering the chest let us give a thought to its smaller brother, the Bible-box, for it fulfilled the worthy purpose of protecting the family Bible and so was another expression of the religious feeling of the settlers. In many instances it acted as a desk. In construction the Bible-boxes vary little from the larger chests, the early ones being oak with wire hinges, which later were supplanted with dovetail hinges affording more beauty and better wear. Rarely was a Bible-box graced with a lock, probably because the theft of a Bible was an unheard-of thing. When the slant lid appears upon them we find that they have almost entirely lost their distinction as receptables for the holy book, and we can imagine that they became storage places for writing implements and papers, for it is on these later boxes that the lock appears to safeguard cherished documents. On some of the lids we find small thumbnail moldings to support the cumbersome volumes which were printed at the time.

It is interesting to note that while the English covered both front and ends with carving, an American Bible-box with carved ends is an almost unheard-of thing. The patterns used followed those of the larger chests with rosettes, sunflowers, and lunettes, though usually put on in higher relief.

This box evolved into the desk-on-a-frame, and when the latter began to appear the former lost its prestige and was eventually thrown into discard.

We must not forget that many of the finest chests were found in Connecticut, and we may attribute this to the fact that the isolation of the

Connecticut colony caused its inhabitants to harbor the old English traditions when the Massachusetts settlers were being informed at irregular intervals of the fads and fancies then rife in England. Yet because of its immediate origin we take the license of classifying the Connecticut chest with Pilgrim furniture.

Before turning our attentions to the chest of drawers let us talk for a while of the desk-on-a-frame, which later merged with the chest of drawers to produce that best-known of all antiques, the highboy. We can trace a very probable line from the Bible-box grown large and cumbersome to the chest-on-a-frame, which, in turn, time and usage would naturally change

WALNUT DESK WITH CABRIOLE LEGS

to a desk, serving a more utilitarian and practical purpose. Many of these desks were made of pine and maple, though the rarer ones are of walnut. The heavy lid edged with a splendid thumbnail molding was usually held in place by dovetail hinges incorrectly called "butterfly" hinges. Sound construction, flush drawers, and unusually heavy dovetailing were the chief characteristics of this piece of furniture. The earliest desks contained a drawer in the carcass of the desk proper, and in later examples we sometimes find a drawer in the frame as well.

The interiors were simple, consisting of a row of pigeonholes, occasionally in the more elaborate examples with small drawers beneath. When there are two drawers in the desk we find the front falls forward instead of lifting up and rests on a pull at either side, as in the slant-top variety.

WALNUT DESK WITH BALL FEET AND WELL

The want of space led to the adding of drawers in the frame and in time to the slant-top desk.

This created a desk of the plainest type with little if any embellishment. A naïve conception of secrecy led to the placing of a well inside the carcass, occupying the space that the top drawer would otherwise have

CHEST-ON-A-FRAME WITH SCRATCH CARVING

15

filled and reached by a sliding panel beneath the pigeonholes. The pigeon-holes usually numbered seven, including a large and pretentious door in the center, which let down to disclose an inner secret compartment. The row of pigeonholes was flanked on the outside by three drawers recessed one above the other. Adjoining was a partition that was scrolled and projected out as far as the front of the well. The front face of the top drawer of course was stationary because the well was behind it, but to all appearance it was workable. We find square pulls to support the lid placed in the upper outside corners. Beneath the false drawer two small drawers were placed, and below we find two longer drawers terminating in a frame supported by bun feet. The drawers as well as the front face of the slanting side which supports the lid were outlined by a double half-round molding. The brasses of these desks, like those of the early highboys, were generally drops, and it is not until in the later piece of mahogany, cherry, pine, and maple that the willow brasses appear.

These early desks were made usually of walnut or were faced with walnut veneer, depending upon their merit. In the later desks the bun feet were replaced by the ball and claw or the bracket feet. The well has also disappeared and we find four full-width drawers. The interiors were usually of the same general type and varied only to suit the fancies of their makers.

One very interesting type of desk which seems to have been comparatively uncommon has small square drawers to support the lid. These drawers were made for candles and they no doubt served their purpose admirably. Many other slight variations occur in these desks, but, as a whole, they were from the start built for use and the simplest and sturdiest construction was employed. It is largely for this reason that so many of them have survived years of hard usage.

The evolution of a chest-on-a-frame to a high chest of drawers is but one short step. Just why the name of highboy has swamped the original name seems to be a mystery, for it was not generally used in the old wills and inventories. These pieces were impressive in most part, yet in some ways

TRUMPET-FOOT HIGHBOY WITH SECRET DRAWER
MOLDING AT TOP

A SPANISH-FOOT HIGHBOY

they did not completely serve the purpose for which they were intended. They were constructed to give additional space to the chest-on-a-frame and as they grew taller they became awkward in size and the top drawers were not serviceable because they were above the reach. It is for this reason that we find two or three drawers used at the top in order to distribute the weight that would naturally have been concentrated in a single top drawer.

With all their beauty and impressiveness, the construction was weak and we find the legs have broken in many cases because they could not support the weight above them. This is more true of the cabriole leg that had no support or brace near the floor, and in proportion many more of the six-legged highboys of the William and Mary type have survived, because their legs were braced on the bottom by stretchers, making for more sound construction. The cabriole leg, without doubt, was a refinement of the six-legged type and, like many improvements, was carried so far as to make the construction subordinate to the outlines.

Let us analyze one of the early six-legged highboys found in this country. The base was supported by six legs, four of which were on the front. A stretcher cut in graceful cyma curves ran between the legs on the four sides. The legs themselves were skilfully turned, piercing the stretcher and terminating in ball feet. The apron of the base is so cut as to give a pleasing silhouette and to take away all severity of line that would have been present if it had run parallel to the drawer sills. The herringbone veneer around drawer fronts gives this piece an air of sophistication and the half-round molding that completely outlines the drawers gives a note of accent.

The base contains a middle drawer of rectangular shape flanked by square drawers on either side. The top, which is slightly set in from the base by moldings, has three large drawers which diminish in depth as they near the top, above which we find two end-to-end drawers.

These pieces are usually about sixty inches in height and the outside length of the table molding is forty inches, with a depth from front to back of twenty-two inches.

In construction and outline the tops of these highboys are much alike,

HIGHBOY WITH BROKEN ARCH AND
QUEEN ANNE LEGS

and we find the bases alone showing the influence of local makers. There are many examples that warrant our study, one of which, of a very early type, has five Flemish legs that in many respects resemble the scroll base of the late Victorian furniture. The piece itself is made of oak and the legs of maple, which justifies the belief that it was made in this country. In

TRUMPET-FOOT HIGHBOY OF WALNUT VENEER WITH
DROP-FRONT SECRETARY TOP

20

HERRINGBONE HIGHBOY WITH CROSS STRETCHER

A DUTCH *KAS* WITH APPLIED MOLDING AND BALL FEET

the five-legged type of highboy as well as the scroll-leg type, the base has no cut-out apron and contains but one drawer. It is very probable that this type was the first advance from the chest-on-frame.

Another variation of a highboy base is found when a cross stretcher appears connecting the legs and a turned finial at the crossing of the stretchers. The brasses of these pieces were usually drops with large

PINE SETTLE

PANELED OAK SETTEE

escutcheon plates, but in later examples willow-pattern handles appear. From this six-legged construction, the Queen Anne or cabriole leg appeared, with the graceful swing of the leg terminating in a swollen

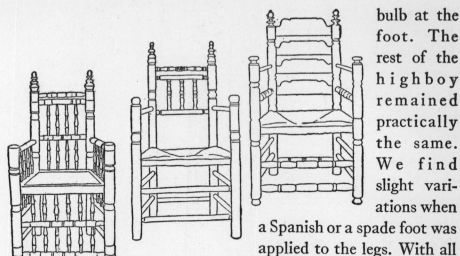

bulb at the foot. The rest of the highboy remained practically the same. We find slight variations when a Spanish or a spade foot was applied to the legs. With all the shortcomings of the high chests their designs have not been improved upon, and we find them reproduced by every large furniture company to-day.

Interesting as the evolution of the highboy from the chest may be let us not overlook the development of the chair from the same source. A glance will convince the most doubtful that the early wainscot chair is not far removed from the Jacobean chest which preceded it in England. A low back on later chests of this era made seats and eventually settles of them, and the construction of the wainscot chair varies little from that of these chest seats. You will notice that the top rail is mortised between the posts and that the panels of the back are set in in the same manner and edged with the same molding as those of the chest. When we come to the legs we find the same

DEVELOPMENT OF THE CHAIR

turnings as
those the
chest-on-a-
frame boast-
ed, as well as
the similar-
ity of con-
struction
which we
have already
mentioned.

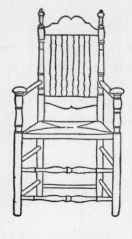

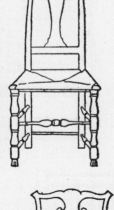

We know that wainscot chairs
were the proudest possession of the household
and surprisingly few in number in the early days, when
a chair was a symbol of wealth, and only to be occupied by the head of the home. Many old inventories
list crimson velvet cushions to relieve the hardness of
the wooden seats that are found in these chairs.

The wainscot chair was rare in this country owing
largely to the fact that it was being replaced in England during the latter part of the Seventeenth Century
by a lighter type of chair, which was more widely copied
by the colonists. The few authentic wainscots of American make lacked the ornate carving so characteristic
of the English type, but in construction were identical
with the latter. The Cromwellian chair, a smaller
edition of the wainscot, was more common here and
may be found in a variety of woods and styles. Many
were turned similarly to the wainscots and others

FROM PILGRIM ERA TO 1800

WAINSCOT CHAIR OF OAK

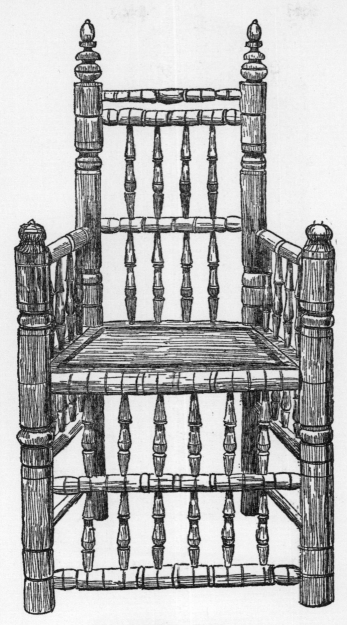

CARVER CHAIR

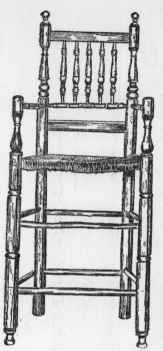

LIGHT CARVER
SIDE CHAIR

CHILD'S HIGH CARVER
CHAIR

LIGHT CARVER ARM-
CHAIR

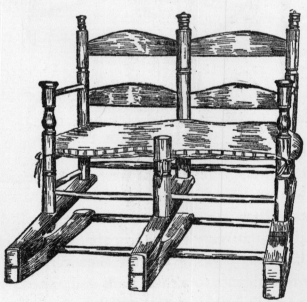

WAGON SEAT

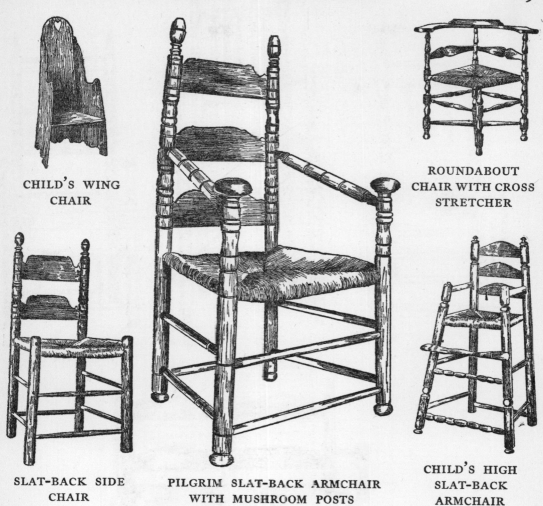

CHILD'S WING
CHAIR

ROUNDABOUT
CHAIR WITH CROSS
STRETCHER

SLAT-BACK SIDE
CHAIR

PILGRIM SLAT-BACK ARMCHAIR
WITH MUSHROOM POSTS

CHILD'S HIGH
SLAT-BACK
ARMCHAIR

boasted sausage turnings. The backs were sometimes solid panels, often covered with leather, velvet, or turkey work.

The names of Brewster and Carver have been applied indiscriminately to a group of chairs that vary so much in appearance as almost to warrant separate classification. What we call the Brewster type received its name from a remote resemblance to a chair made and owned by Elder Brewster. These chairs were the height of accomplishment of the woodturner's art,

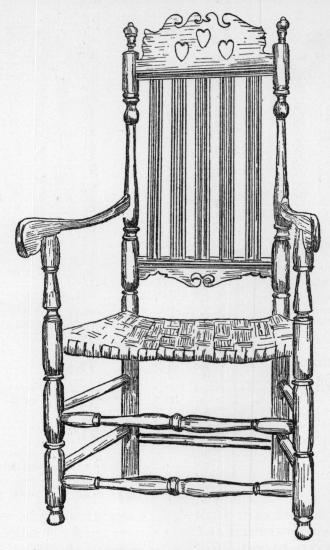

BANNISTER-BACK CHAIR WITH HEART
AND CROWN DECORATION

having a row of spindles under either arm, a double row forming the back, and a single or double row beneath the seat rail. Ash was the best available wood for turning, and hence we find the majority of the Brewster type

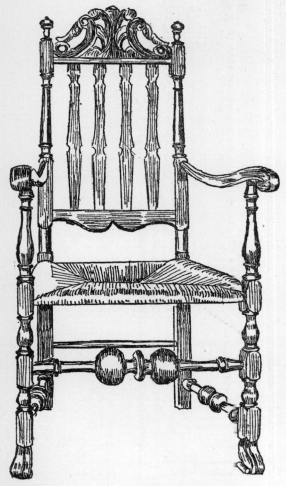

BANNISTER-BACK ARMCHAIR WITH
SPANISH FEET, BULBOUS TURNINGS,
AND CARVED TOPRAIL

BANNISTER-BACK SIDE CHAIR
WITH CARVED
TOPRAIL

chairs made of it. The back posts ran to the floor to form the legs and were
capped with heavy ball finials seemingly best fitted to the sturdy construction of the chair. The line of the arm was carried through the back in the
center rail which supported the two rows of spindles. It can readily be
supposed that this overabundance of turnings did not make for much com-

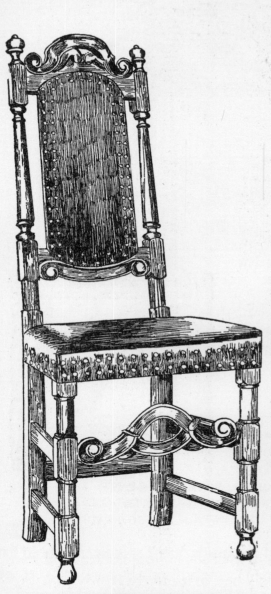

CARVED FLEMISH CHAIR WITH
LEATHER BACK

CARVED FLEMISH CHAIR WITH
CANE BACK AND SEAT

32

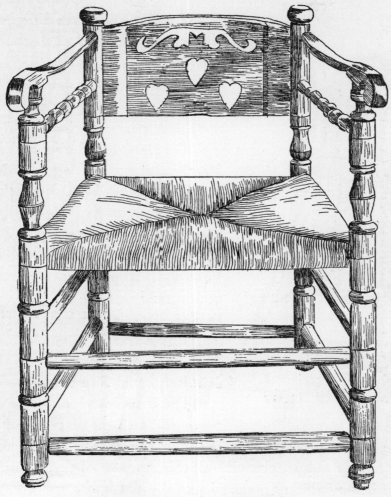

CONNECTICUT ARMCHAIR WITH SECONDARY
SAUSAGE TURNINGS AND HEART AND
CROWN DECORATION

fort and we find in many cases that the inside of the spindles has been flattened. The seats of these chairs varied, some having wooden panels set into the seat frame while others were rushed or covered with leather.

As time goes on we find the Brewster chair becoming lighter in construction and hence more popular for general use, although the massiveness

CHILD'S WINDSOR CHAIR

of the earlier type gave a dignity which was lacking in the later chairs. Fewer as well as thinner spindles helped in making the chair less cumbersome, and in many cases the spindles beneath the seat and arms disappeared entirely.

The slat-back chair was distinctly a Pilgrim century innovation, and the style has persisted until the present day. The first of these chairs had simple straight posts with three or more slats across the back, first straight and later spooned. Variations creep in when we find secondary turned stretchers, serpentine or shaped slats, and when the front leg meets the arm in a mushroom crown. The arm is sometimes flat and other times delicately molded or turned.

The bannister-back came in simultaneously with the slat- or ladder-back. To be sure they were more aristocratic in appearance, and boasted more grace and beauty of line, yet with all this, because of their stiffness, they never gained the ordinary popularity of the slat-back.

The Flemish chairs with their elaborate carved outline were found only in the finest homes in America and more often than not were imported rather than locally made. At the beginning of the Eighteenth Century many of the homes in this country rivaled those of England in luxury, and it is in these homes that we find Flemish chairs of English origin appearing. To be sure, they could not be imported in any numbers without affecting local cabinetworkers who depended upon foreign fads and fancies as the inspiration in their own output, and we may say for certain that

WINDSOR

Hoop-back with Comb
1725 - 1750

High bow-back, arm
1730 - 1760

Comb-back, arm
1730 - 1750

Brace-Bow-back
1725 - 1750

Writing-Arm, Roundabout
1750 - 1800

Eight Legged Settee 1750-1775

Fan-back
1750 - 1775

Flemish chairs were made in America. Usually of maple or the fruit woods, they were elaborately and skilfully carved in the ram's horn arms, in the bold scrolled back, and in the front stretcher, which was mortised and tenoned to the front legs. A fine caned panel was set into the back and the seat.

Although this chair was in vogue at the same time as the slat-back, we must dissociate it from the cruder farmhouse furniture and consider it in connection with the furniture of the wealthier and better-furnished homes of the cities.

We must not leave the discussion of chairs without considerable mention of the Windsor, which though English in origin was perfected and carried in this country to a stage of development which far surpassed the English Windsor at its best. It was our native craftsmen who foresaw in this chair unlimited possibilities for grace and delicacy without sacrificing strength, and the result was a variety of Windsors, hoop-back, fan-back, brace-back, roundabout, and writing-arm, that warrant a book for their description alone. Although later in period, we venture to include them in this chapter.

In general construction there is little deviation in the various types. The bow back, legs, and seat were worked while the wood was green so that when the wood shrank all joints would automatically tighten. Also the green wood could be bent with little danger of breaking, particu-

WINDSOR CHAIR WITH BAMBOO TURNING

WINDSOR STOOL

larly the hickory that was used for the bow. The seat was usually of pine and the legs were forced into holes driven through the seat and held securely by a peg forced through the leg from the top, splitting the leg and wedging it in a fashion that would remove all chance of weakness. As seat and bow shrank their hold on the spindles tightened and made a unit more solid than glue could ever have done. For the bow and hoop we sometimes find that ash or white oak was substituted for hickory, although the latter is more common. The turned legs and stretchers were usually of maple, most adaptable to this purpose.

The grace of line and sturdy construction of the Windsor chair make it one of our most interesting studies. Some of us show preference for the refined line of the high bow-back, while to others the solidity of the writing-arm Windsor is more appealing. The seats of these chairs are cut in irregular shape to make a place for the spindles which support the writing-arm. The arm itself is broadened to make a support for the arm and paper and displays a boxlike structure below containing one or two drawers.

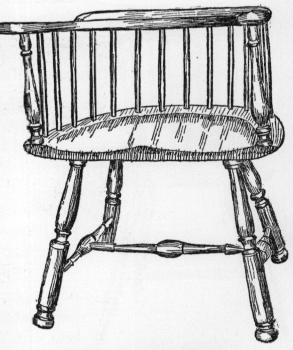

WINDSOR TABLE   HEAVY ROUNDABOUT WINDSOR CHAIR

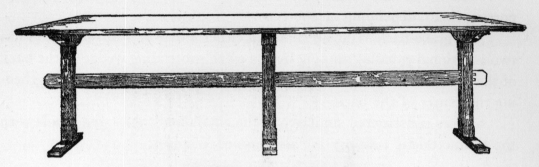

TRESTLE BOARD TABLE

HUTCH TABLE OF PINE

The backs are of the bow or comb variety with any number of spindles supporting them, depending on the type.

The brace-back Windsor comes in either a bow or a fan-back and has two additional spindles running from a small protruding wedge at the back of the seat into the bow between the regular spindles, thereby strengthening the center of the back.

Settees constructed similarly to the chairs and tables and stools with the characteristic turnings are also termed Windsor.

The trestle table, the immortal board at which many of the English heroes have been pictured, has been carried down to us through the Pilgrim Fathers. Warriors, kings, or Puritans, it served them all alike, and seemed to reflect their rugged spirit. Perhaps it was the sturdiness that appealed to the English, but it seems likely to suppose that the simplicity of construction was the feature that won the hearts of our forefathers.

It could be easily fashioned from rough boards with little of the knowledge of a skilled craftsman or of skill with his tools. The top was a large board some thirty-six inches wide supported by two trestle legs resembling a double-headed T. For added strength a center stretcher was used and spindles that ran upright from the stretcher to the top gave the longer

STRETCHER TABLE

TURNED MEDIAL STRETCHER TABLE

tables more solidity. These tables are very rare, for they are few in number and those that have escaped the woodpile in their many years of disuse are now treasured by museums and collectors.

In the old inventories we find listings of many maple trenchers and bowls that were used with this type of table. They were round plates which now, due to the shrinking of the wood, give an appearance of being slightly oval. The size varied according to the use in the household. The larger trenchers were as deep as two inches with a diameter of twelve inches, whereas the smaller plates, which have been found in greater numbers, had a depth of one half inch and a seven and a half inch diameter. The shrinkage of as much as an inch is often noted in a twelve-inch plate.

STRETCHER TABLE WITH HIGH, EGG-TURNED STRETCHERS

The form of the smaller trenchers greatly resembled that of the pewter plates that followed them. It can be easily supposed that they were put on a hand-turning lathe that quickly could fashion out this simplest and most economical substitute for pewter or silver.

To come back to the trestle table, it was made to fit local requirements, varied in length, and often boasted some construction to add strength or to fill some unique household need.

We must not overlook the hutch table, which also had great merit in its simplicity of construction, and more than that, in its compactness, which made it so popular in the homes of our forefathers. These tables were usually made of pine, with oval, round, or square tops of sufficient size to seat as many as six people. The tops were of wide boards held fast on the under side by two heavy cross-pieces. These cross-pieces hinged on a wooden peg at the side of the box, making the top tiltable. The frame of the box was usually dovetailed at its edges and terminated in shoes. It is possible that these tables were inspired by a wainscot chair or chest. They were fashioned of pine, making them light in weight and easily pushed

SMALL TRUMPET-FOOT TABLE WITH TILE TOP AND CROSS STRETCHERS

SMALL TRESTLE TABLE

STRETCHER TABLE WITH FLAT MEDIAL STRETCHER

back against a wall. When the top was turned back the table served the twofold purpose of a seat and storage space. The top of the seat was sometimes fastened to the frame by wire hinges. When the top was lifted the box served as a receptacle for the kitchen ware, such as spoons, plates, and bits of linen. The sides were scrolled above the molded shoes. The more elaborate and later tables had beneath the seat one and in some cases two drawers. These drawers came into use about the same time that they appear in chests. When economy of space was no longer the essential requirement in the home furnishings hutch tables were supplemented by a refectory type.

As early as 1630 the refectory tables appear in oak. They were sturdy in construction, and in many cases were used not only in the home, but as

BUTTERFLY TABLE OF MAPLE

TRESTLE TABLE WITH FLAT GATE

communion tables for the church. The turnings were of the simplest type, without any reminiscence of the bulbous Jacobean turnings and carved legs that appeared in England. Oak was soon discarded because maple was found to be the better wood for the turned legs and stretchers and the shaped apron, while the top could easily be made of pine. These tables have served us through many years because of their faultless construction. A variation may be found in the center stretcher type, which usually had a turned stretcher, although in many of the other tables we find them flat. The medial stretcher corresponded in turnings to the legs and pinned itself

CRANE BRACKET BUTTERFLY TABLE

GATE-LEG TABLE WITH FLAT GATES

into the square block in the turned stretcher which connected the front and back legs. This table was probably devised because the side stretchers of the refectory type of table made it impossible to bring a chair close

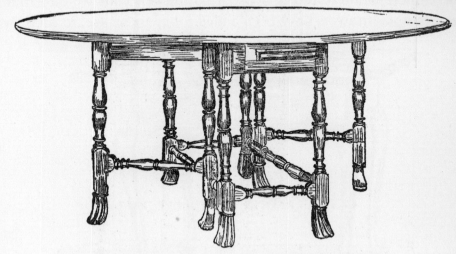

GATE-LEG TABLE WITH SPANISH FEET

GATE-LEG TABLE

enough to the table to eat with comfort. The top of the table usually projected twice as far at the ends as it did over the sides. This was done to offset the inconvenience of the stretcher.

The earliest of these tables boasted no drawers, but we find that in the later examples drawers have been added for convenience, to tuck away

CABRIOLE-LEG TABLE WITH SCROLLED APRON

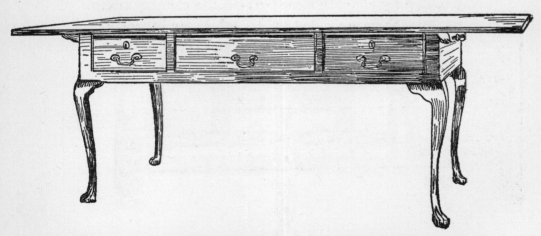

WALNUT TABLE WITH CABRIOLE LEGS AND THREE DRAWERS

CANDLESTAND WITH
X BASE

the many things that littered up the small rooms. In different parts of the country, local variations will be found. Occasionally the tops have the same construction as the hutch table and hinge with a large peg, which is placed through the apron of the table on either side.

A dough-kneading trough is another variation of the tables found in early homes. This table may have a top like the hutch or it may slide off at either side. When the top is removed it discloses a well-shaped box in which dough was kneaded; hence the name. This well was made by lengthening the apron and fixing a bottom to it.

Perhaps it was the inconvenience of the stretcher, or perhaps the lack of space, that led to the devising of drop leaves on various types of tables. Naturally they had to have some definite support, and we find the simple beginnings of the gate-leg table.

At first the leaf was upheld by a solid scrolled support called a butter-fly wing. In some parts of the country tradition tells us these are called rudder tables, and the wing is said to be a discarded rudder of a boat reversed in position to support the leaf.

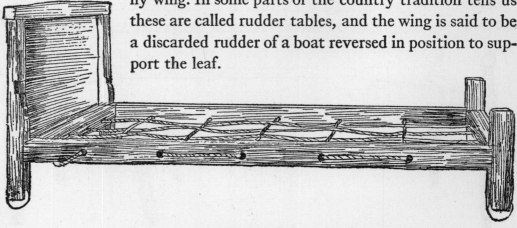

TRUNDLE BED

The stretcher table also added a flat gate and in some instances a crane bracket to support the leaf. As a rule these tables were small, about twenty-five inches high, with a top of an elliptical shape, approximately twenty-five by thirty-five. We can easily imagine from their smallness that they were incidental tables in the home.

We must not overlook the small trestle table that had two heavily turned end-posts terminating in scrolled shoes and a base almost as wide as the shoe that ran between the two legs. A flat pivot gate was inserted in this board. The tops were usually oval or square, with the edges turned, and, lacking an apron, these tables never contained drawers. The height of the table was approximately twenty-seven inches, with a two-inch gate to support the top. They were made in oak, cherry, maple, and pine. The single, folding gate-leg table was probably another derivation of this type. The flat gate now became more elaborate and displayed the same turnings as the legs. With this change it can be readily seen that the simple tavern table has evolved into the gate-leg type.

TRIPOD CANDLE-
STAND WITH
SCREW TOP

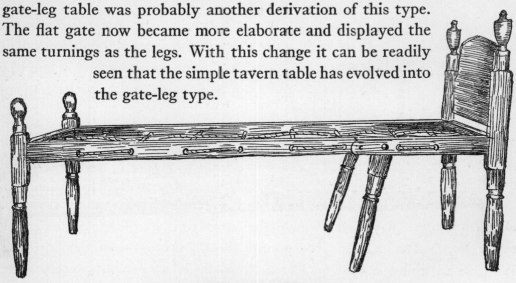

FOLDING PRESS BED

FOLDING BED WITH CRANE HEAD

The great variety of gate-leg tables was due to the ingenuity of the craftsmen. Each tried to outdo the other, and from the simple idea of the gate-leg table with the flat gates they skilfully constructed tables with as many as four gates. It must be remembered that in terminology the "single gate-leg table" has two gates and the "four gate-leg table" has two gates on either side.

Even the smaller tables, such as the candlestands, were developed with originality, yet each retained the characteristics of one of the larger types. We find the trestle table, adapted with the cross-stretcher base, the Windsor turnings, and so on. Often these pieces were merely smaller replicas of their bigger brothers. They served as incidental tables beside the bed or in the living room, to hold such lighting equipment as was used at the time. The posts are chamfered or skilfully turned, terminating in a molded foot and topped by a round or square top.

The ingenious candlestands show great variation from a simple shaft with a round top into a mere mechanical appliance with a ratchet slide or a screw shaft. These we shall treat at greater length in the chapter on lighting equipment.

The exact form of the earliest beds used in this country is problematical, but we can feel assured that they were very simple and included in the construction of the house. You will recall that the Pilgrims at Plymouth built their first huts on the side of a hill, which makes us wonder if perhaps beds of pine boughs were not their first resting places. To be sure, a bed such as this was only used in the rough huts, and as they made their log cabins, they no doubt built their beds actually into the walls.

We must resort to the earliest inventories, and here we find only the listings of such things as mattresses filled with rush, cushions, pillows, and other furniture, but we never find in the earlier years a mention of a bed. This would almost prove that the bed was in some way an architectural part of the house; in other words, a mere bunk raised from the floor by boards, with a mattress resting on boughs or rush, and curtained for

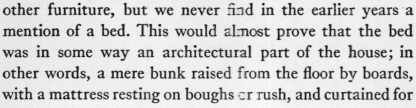

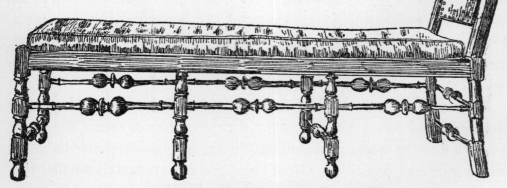

TURNED EIGHT-LEGGED DAY BED

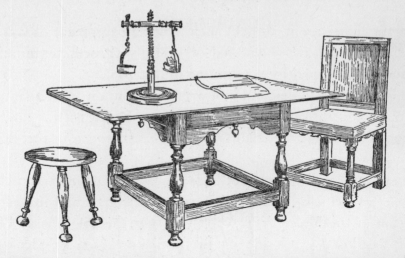

WINDSOR STOOL, STRETCHER TABLE, AND WAINSCOT CHAIR

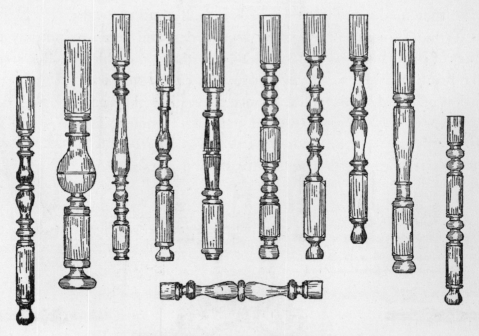

STRETCHER TABLE TURNINGS

CHAIR DETAILS
1630–1800

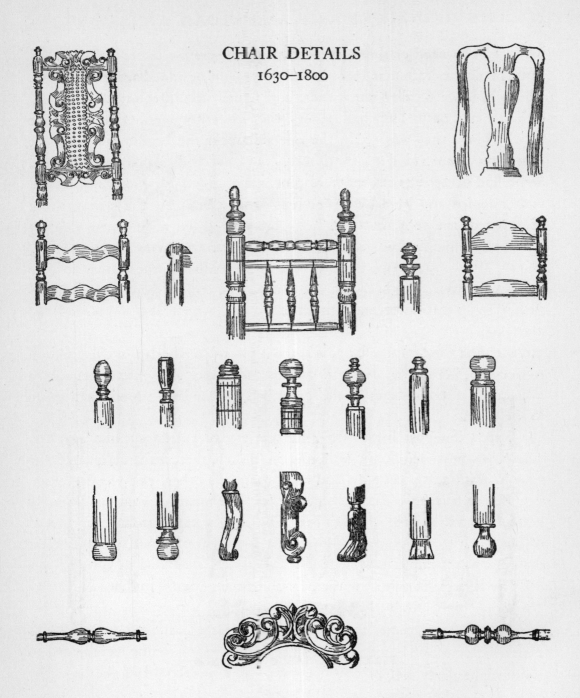

privacy. The need of space, or perhaps the desire for better living conditions, made the craftsman create a bed that might be folded against the wall. These beds were called press beds, and folded up either under a canopy or into a cupboard. They had six legs, the two center ones acting as a brace for the hinge that was set in the side rails near the headboard. As more chambers were added to the house, four-post beds came into fashion. Some had octagon posts, made of pine, while others were skilfully turned and canopied and were known as tent or field beds. As the ceilings were heightened, the tops that had been flat were given a delightful flourish and a rhythmic line was added to the canopy. Draperies of needlework, chintz, and copper-plate printed toile were added to these beds to give privacy, as well as to keep out the drafts. The earliest beds were held together by tautly stretched, interlaced ropes, which also supported the mattress.

As time went on, the trundle bed with wooden wheels, for the children to sleep on, became an essential part of the home. These little beds were rolled each morning beneath the larger bed, and so used up no extra space in the room.

Later, low-post beds with great variety of turnings came into use. These low-post beds may be found in the characteristic designs of the time in walnut, maple, pine, and cherry and the other fruit woods.

Before leaving beds, let us glance for a moment at what is seemingly a luxury for the time—the day bed. These beds were true in every detail to the furniture types of the time in which they were made, whether their turnings were simple, carved in Flemish style, or molded in Queen Anne cabriole legs. As a rule these beds had eight legs, with the two end posts projecting higher than the seat. These two posts form the construction for the back. Sometimes the back was a movable unit that could be regulated for comfort, but as a rule, splats, spindles, or caning were joined to the upright posts and became an immovable headboard of the bed. The seats were either rushed, laced, or caned.

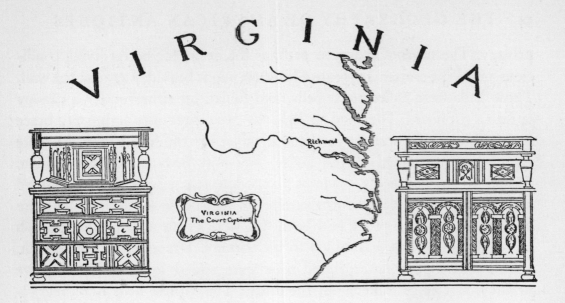

CHAPTER II

OAK FURNITURE AND COURT CUPBOARDS

IN ASSIGNING oak furniture to Virginia we do not intend to convey the idea that such furniture was not produced elsewhere, but in this colony as in no other was the Jacobean tradition preserved in its purity by men in whom it was inherent. The Virginia colony had at the start the backing of a powerful trading company and the advantage of a unique staple crop, tobacco, which was soon to be her chief export. From the days of her first settlement Virginia was a refuge for Royalists, and at the outbreak of the Civil War in England she, with the other southern colonies, profited by the immigration of large groups drawn from the Cavalier and Royalist classes, then in disfavor.

The Jacobean influence had been restricted to the Court and the homes of the great, so it is natural that the men who settled Virginia brought with them the best of the Jacobean tradition, and in their houses as well as in their furniture we find this element predominant for many years.

The typical English country home or manor house of the period was built about a rectangular center section, with low wings at either or one end to give the U or L shape. These homes were constructed in most cases of brick and timber or all of brick, and it is not surprising to find efforts being made in the first years of the establishment of the Jamestown colony to restrict dwellings to brick construction. How successful these efforts were is more than doubtful, for we read that the first entire brick home in Virginia was built in 1638.

A quotation from a narrative concerning the founding of Henrico, Virginia, gives us some information concerning the exteriors of the houses: "and to answer the first objection for holesome lodging, here they have built competent and decent houses, the first stories all of brick," etc. We can see right here an expression of the Jacobean tradition in architecture that I believe will be difficult to duplicate anywhere in New England or in the middle Atlantic colonies. From other descriptions obtained from wills, letters, and similar sources, we may compound a general idea of the interiors of such homes. Low, long rooms, with a center oaken beam or chamfered beams across the entire ceiling, were characteristic. In many rooms rectangular paneling, set into rails and stiles, was used. In other instances the walls were covered with wainscot sheathing. Windows were small and few in number and when they were not filled with small leaded panes there were wooden shutters to keep out the cold.

Furniture in almost every known instance retained rectangular forms and followed with little variation the pure elements of the Jacobean furniture. We know that nearly all of this early furniture in Virginia was made of oak and we could go on indefinitely quoting proof of this from old wills and inventories. But unfortunately for us the extant examples are rarities to-day and we may attribute this to two facts. In the first place, the southern settlers, being men of means and not without position in the mother country, were able to import furniture from England, and as the colonies grew, regular trade brought to these shores furniture made

SERRATED CUPBOARD WITH BULBOUS UPRIGHTS
AND ARCHED CENTER PANEL

abroad. So when a new fad appeared overseas, furniture in use here was thrown into discard and replaced with imports. As a rule the discarded furniture found its way to slave houses and in time was destroyed by hard use.

And so because they were not forced by circumstance to make their own pieces, but inclined rather to import what the mother country was sponsoring at the moment, we to-day must study the furniture of these early Virginians from a very few extant pieces, and more from written records of the times.

So far as we know the range of pieces in this country was similar to that in England and consisted in a large part of chests, tables, a few chairs, many formes, joined stools, cupboards, and state beds.

Throughout this chapter on oak furniture we shall limit our general discussion to that of Virginia, but it must not be supposed that oak furniture was not produced elsewhere. From New England we have many pieces constructed entirely of oak and others in which oak is used in combination with other woods. The oak period of Virginia lasted but a short time and was supplanted by the use of well-known Virginia walnut, but with the introduction of the latter wood, furniture forms changed considerably. In many instances the oak furniture of Virginia varies in form and structure from that produced anywhere else in the colonies and it is most regrettable that through a lack of authenticated pieces in great numbers we are forced in many situations to use our imagination.

Chairs of the period were of the wainscot variety and formal and dignified in appearance. In the armchair type the front legs run up to the arm to form the post, and the seats, as in the side chairs, are of wood. Seat rails were tenoned into the legs, as were the stretchers. Rails were generally heavy on all pieces of furniture, and were mortised and tenoned and pinned together with heavy wooden pegs.

More in use than the chair was the joined stool, resembling in construction and form a small table. The legs ran from a block where they met

JOINT STOOL

the skirt into a short turned member, again into a block to contain the chamfered stretcher, and ended in a small turned foot. The skirt was carved, usually with the guilloche design. Benches known as formes were similar in construction but larger in dimension. Three-legged stools had splayed legs and oval or round tops.

Tables appear in several styles, one similar to the three-legged stool mentioned above, the tavern type, trestle type, and gate-leg. An interesting early Virginia table is of trestle construction with inch-thick wide planks for support at either end. These crude legs run into shoes at the floor and between the shoes runs a flat wide stretcher. At the center of either side is inserted in a small bored hole an H-shaped unturned gate, which sup-

EARLY VIRGINIA COURT CUPBOARD WITH APPLIED CORBELS

OAK TABLE WITH TRUMPET TURNINGS AND GATE
LEGS IN THE FRAME

OAK BUFFET WITH APPLIED MOLDINGS

ports the drop leaves. The construction of this table throughout is of oak.

Another example of early folding tables from Virginia is in the author's collection. This table has six legs, four of which are in the front. The two center front legs bear an unusual construction that permits them to swing out at right angles and support the folding drop leaf. The apron of this table is about six inches deep and the top blocks of the center legs are flush with it when folded. At the top of the skirt this block meets a bar that has been cut free of the skirt and runs to the corner where it pivots on a long peg carved out of the end block and which in turn pegs into the table top. The apron of this table is shaped and the legs are of the William and Mary trumpet type, with shallow turnings. A straight flat stretcher connects the legs.

Cupboards were of four varieties: the hanging cupboard, the wall or corner cupboard, the livery cupboard, and the court cupboard. The first type we can imagine was used for storage space for cloth, dishes, and cooking utensils. In a few cases probably it was used for a food cupboard as well, but we find usually that requirement filled by the so-called livery cupboard. In general, they were paneled with molded stiles and rails and an occasional bit of carving on the top rail or stiles. They varied in size from two and a half to five feet long, the long ones being used as receptacles for clothes.

A livery cupboard in true form is an unusual find in America, and the few examples which exist have never been proven to be of American make. Wills and inventories of early date mention "livery" cupboards, but absence of accurate description leads us to believe that this term was applied to any contrivance made to hold food. In England in the Fifteenth and Sixteenth centuries it had been the custom to give an allotted amount of food and lighting material, ample for the night, to the members of the family, guests, and menials each evening before retiring. This allotment was known as "livery," and a small cupboard in the sleeping room, in which it was stored, was called a "livery cupboard." "Livery" of clothes

OAK PRESS

was only served to inferiors. For proper ventilation and light, turned spindles between upper and lower rails at the sides and front appear rather than panels. In America, the term "livery cupboard" is used in referring not only to the small hanging cupboards but to the court cupboards as well when the latter were used for food storage.

The early English form of court cupboard consisted of four upright

CUPBOARD WITH CARVED TORUS MOLDING AND SPLAYED SIDES

posts with a shelf near the floor, another near the center of the uprights, and a top shelf or hood. This form has never been found in any American cupboard, probably because it had been superseded in England by the enclosed cupboard before the date of early colonizing here. In general, we may divide American court cupboards into three groups. In the first the

OAK PRESS WITH DROP PANEL

upper carcass is enclosed and the lower open, with a shelf between the uprights near the floor. The upper part may have a center fixed panel with doors at either side; a center door with splayed sides; or a center door with splayed sides which also are hinged, making three entrances into the upper carcass. In the second type, a drawer is added below the enclosed upper part and sometimes below the shelf another is placed. The construction of the upper section remains identical throughout all three types. The third and last has an enclosed lower carcass as well as an upper. One drawer is sometimes retained and occasionally the entire lower half is filled with drawers. At other times three doors, flanked by fixed panels, form the base.

One cupboard of this type illustrated was obtained by the author from an old farmhouse in southern Virginia. In the place of doors in the lower carcass is a paneled drop front with a Jacobean knob and escutcheon. The uprights between the two members are more delicate than is usual, and both capitals and fluting of the fixed panels of the upper section bespeak English rather than American origin. The piece rests upon large ball feet and is constructed throughout of oak. This type of cupboard with both parts enclosed is more correctly called press cupboard.

The turnings of the upright supports throughout all the cupboards are truly Jacobean, either the bulbous or spiral type. Corbels, channel moldings, billeted, serrated, or carved moldings, triglyphs, arched panels, scratch carving, turning, and painting are all employed in making the court and press cupboards the most elaborate pieces of the time.

Two splendid examples are on display in the American Wing of the Metropolitan Museum, in New York City. One is a true court cupboard with a heavy shelf near the floor, bulbous turned members between the shelf and drawer as well as at the ends of the upper carcass. The two doors of the enclosed section are beautifully paneled and between them a fixed center panel bears an unusual arch with considerable architectural quality. The skirt of the shelf is shaped below the molding. Corbels appear on the spaces at the ends and between the two drawers, as well as at either side of the permanent panel of the upper part. The turned uprights are heavier at the top than at the bottom. A serrated molding runs about the top of the hood broken in the center and at the ends by applied corbels.

The other cupboard in the same collection is of the press variety. Two large doors appear in the lower half and the drawer beneath the center shelf is omitted. In the upper half two doors appear at either side of a center panel. This panel, the doors of both upper and lower carcasses, and the rail of the hood are elaborately carved and paneled. The two lower doors and the center panel above display the arch, and the end panels and the space inside the arches bear scratch carving.

The Brooklyn Museum owns a splendid and unusual cupboard of peculiar construction. A deep torus molding runs below the shelf and is decorated with a double band of foliate carving. The same design appears on the rail of the hood, with corbels placed at the ends and center. The doors of the lower section are free of any embellishment aside from small bosses in the centers of the door panels and corbels on the stiles, while the door and splayed sides of the upper part are paneled and bear bosses and corbels in greater numbers. The turning of the uprights is not particularly pleasing in this piece.

SUNFLOWER COURT CUPBOARD WITH
APPLIED CORBELS

In the Yale University collection is a cupboard most ornate in style and decoration. The sunflower and tulip designs so common on chests and Bible-boxes are used in profusion on the center door of the lower carcass and the fixed panels which flank it. The doors and panels of the upper part are treated in a very decorative manner with corbels and bosses in large numbers. The supporting upright members are deeply turned in beautiful lines.

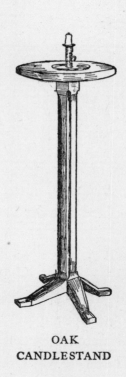

OAK
CANDLESTAND

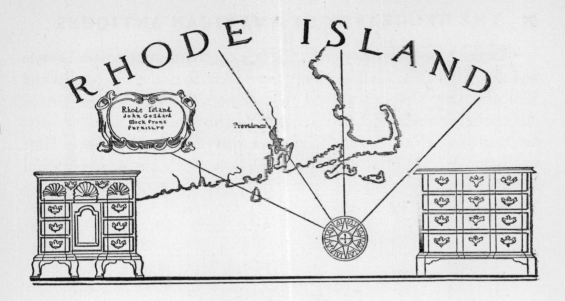

CHAPTER III

GODDARD AND THE BLOCK FRONT

BLOCK-FRONT pieces may be defined as those on which the front face is relieved with a sunken panel flanked on either side by raised blocks that terminate at the base in a molded bracket foot and are sometimes topped with a shell design.

John Goddard, stylist and greatest exponent of block-front furniture, was born in Newport, and became perhaps America's greatest craftsman. Although he did not originate this type of furniture, as many claim, he did develop it and carry it to perfection, and he is the only American cabinetworker whose name is associated with certainty with block-front furniture. Just when and where this style was created is problematical, but we know of several extant examples that were created by skilled English workers of the Queen Anne period.

The Chippendale influence that was overrunning the colonies at this time touched John Goddard lightly but never completely swamped his personality and excellent craftsmanship. His style we may justly say was

69

BLOCK-FRONT BUREAU

more substantial than Chippendale's, and surely more so than that of the imitators of the great craftsmen who were working throughout the country. Newport, even at this early date, was a wealthy seaport, and its luxurious homes were filled with imported and the best locally made pieces, the former of which no doubt often inspired Goddard.

The shop of Job Townsend, situated also in Newport, was the scene of Goddard's first activities, for he worked there at an early age and in later years married Townsend's daughter. Sixteen children were born to them, but only one followed his father's profession, and even this one

BLOCK-FRONT DESK

never became a skilled craftsman. While working for Townsend, Goddard first attempted block-front furniture, but it was crude experimenting. In many of these early attempts we find that the block is very shallow, scarcely raised above the carcass of the piece, and that the shell motif is missing. In general, the early block fronts lacked the refined finish that the later pieces boasted as one of their greatest charms.

Goddard produced many pieces of furniture without this block front that so characterizes him. Let us take, for example, a highboy attributed

BLOCK-FRONT BROKEN ARCH SECRETARY

72

with considerable authenticity to his workshop. In this example all influence of Chippendale has been swept aside and the graceful spirit of the Queen Anne predominates. To be sure, in the rhythmic lines of the apron we find the shell motif swinging gracefully into a simple cabriole leg, but the general lines of the carcass of the piece, as well as most of the decorative detail of its embellishments, is of a period earlier than Chippendale. The base contains three small drawers side by side and above them a long drawer extending the full length of the piece. The top has three large drawers and above them centered a small square drawer with two smaller rectangular drawers flanking it. Above these is a large panel that follows in line and accents the broken pediment. A carved flame appears at either end and in the center of the arch. Plain brasses complete the piece, adding another note of perfect dignity.

As time went on Goddard, working at the block front, deepened the blocks and elaborated the shell carving, which so successfully counteracted the perpendicular lines that predominated in the desk. When three blocks appear on his furniture the inner one is concave and the outer ones convex, with the shell corresponding. Not only was this shell an integral part of the design, but the bracket foot was blocked, carrying the blocking treatment down through the molding into the foot.

An ingenious expression of Goddard's love of grace is seen in the rosette design at the arch of the pediment, which revolves and thereby leads the eye back along the flowing line of the pediment.

In the knee-hole desk the center panel was set far enough back to make room for the knees when sitting before it, but the blocking was identical with that of the straight-front desks, or omitted in the center section and replaced with a plain panel. This panel was hinged and when opened disclosed a row of drawers or shelves. Many of these desks were ornamented with pierced Chippendale handles, which no doubt were imported from England or reproduced in Goddard's shop.

In the tall desks of this craftsman strength and dignity prevailed, and

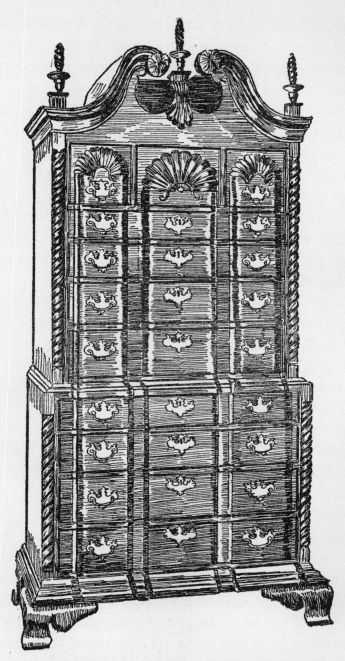

BROKEN ARCH BLOCK-FRONT CHEST-ON-CHEST

74

the illusion of additional height was given by the repetition of the perpendicular line. A broken arch pediment added still more to this effect. The door fronts of the upper section followed unerringly the blocking of the desk front and lid. The three blocks of the upper carcass are divided so that the left front hinges on the side of the body and the middle panel is hinged to the panel at the right, which was in turn again hinged to the right side of the body. So, the left panel swung free, the center panel alone could swing out, or the center and right-hand panels could swing clear out together. This method of hinging was also reversed.

Candle-pulls were added to these tall desks to furnish a place for lighting equipment. A half-round fluted column broke the severe line of the corners of the upper part and converging shells decorated the small drawers on the inside of the desk.

Just a word about the actual construction of block-front furniture. Contrary to the predominating belief, the block and shell in many cases were applied and not made from a solid piece. In many of the three block pieces the outer or concave shell was glued in place while the center or convex shell was carved from the same solid piece as the block part itself.

It is interesting to note that Goddard, in spite of all his earnest efforts and skilled craftsmanship, died bankrupt, and in the short space of one hundred and fifty years his furniture is bringing among the highest prices paid for any American antiques. Unlike many cabinetmakers, he did not put labels on his furniture, which makes it difficult to-day to trace with authenticity actual examples of his handiwork.

Throughout Connecticut, Massachusetts, and New Hampshire we find random examples of block-front furniture, some of which no doubt came from the Newport shop of John Goddard, and some of which was certainly made by other unknown craftsmen who recognized the decorative possibilities of the block front and attempted to manufacture it for their own clientèle. In almost every case, however, they did so with little or no æsthetic success.

The details that Goddard employed in his furniture, as well as his foresight in creating unity and strength with the use of upright lines terminating in molded feet or a broken arch, won him his laurels.

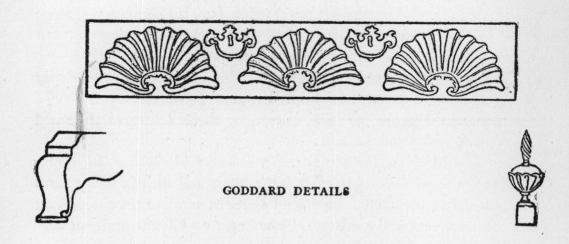

GODDARD DETAILS

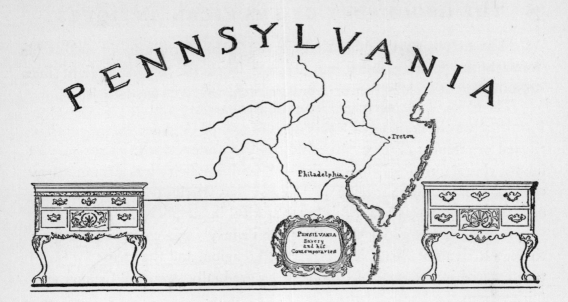

CHAPTER IV

SAVERY AND HIS CONTEMPORARIES

PENNSYLVANIA was never lacking in able craftsmen. Whether in glass, metal, or the furniture crafts, they excelled in their particular trades. Perhaps it was the combination of racial inheritances and religious influences that made this colony so different from New England and the others, yet so interesting in an individual way.

The furniture of Pennsylvania may be divided into three large classes: The first group includes that brought into this country by William Penn and his followers, and that made by them in the earliest years of the colony. Of this furniture we know little aside from the fact that it must have been of English or German derivation or a mixture of the two.

The second class must be separated for intelligent study into farmhouse and city furniture. Going back to New England, we know that the seaboard cities were kept in constant touch with the mother country and that there styles were copied from up-to-date importations. In contrast, the settlers who had pushed far inland depended for inspiration upon the faint memories of the homeland which of necessity became distorted by the urgent need for household equipment of any sort.

The cities of Pennsylvania boasted great wealth and beautiful homes. Furniture was in keeping with this spirit of refined elegance, but the sophisticated ornateness of later pieces was as yet undeveloped. Thrift was an inborn characteristic of the Quaker sect, and simplicity was demanded by their religion; to these specific qualities we may attribute the phenomenon of furniture that was beautiful, but beautiful in simplicity.

A wave of prosperity that swept the Pennsylvania colony about 1750, the new arrivals of varied nationality and religion, and the vogue for furniture created in the style of Chippendale, gradually swept all Quaker simplicity from the homes of the colony.

The furniture that follows that turning point constitutes our third classification; it was indirectly a mere outgrowth of what had preceded, and was confined strictly to city products. The farmhouse furniture varies little down through the years. English cabinetmakers coming to Philadelphia brought Chippendale designs, and nowhere in the colonies were better interpretations of this great craftsman made than in Philadelphia.

The craftsmen of this city not only watched foreign cabinetworkers but, being shrewd, they also watched their own competitors with vigilance. Possibly jealousy prompted this, but we know that they did not allow the workers of other cities to ruin their trade by underselling. As early as 1742 there was published in the Philadelphia *Gazette* an enlightening advertisement which proves this trade jealousy. They were Plunket Fleeson's easy-flowing words, assuring us that, "Several sorts of good chair frames, black and red leather, may be had, finished cheaper than any made here or imported from Boston." This was not the first mention of red leather in this use for, in 1729, the *American Weekly Mercury* sketches the latest fad of the time, "the startling use of red leather to upholster the seats and backs of chairs." This was well before Chippendale's advocating this material for the same use, and though it is doubtful that his inspiration came from the colonies, it is logical to suppose that the colonists established the fad in this country before it gained a firm foothold in England.

The furniture of early Philadelphia craftsmen, although simple in character and lacking the ornate carving and splendid finish which we usually connect with pieces from that city, nevertheless differed from that of other sections of the country in that as early as 1738 we find the use of exotic woods. To quote an announcement of a sale of that date: "local as well as woods of the West Indies can be purchased as well as a parcel of choice curly maple." It is only logical that the importation of exotic woods would lead to the creation of furniture far more sophisticated than the provincial country types. With the advent of more skilled labor we find wholesale firms established and offering to the trade such wares as "mahogany and walnut tea table columns." This advertisement from a Philadelphia *Chronicle* of 1769 goes on to assure us that with the given parts the mere matter of assembling could quickly be accomplished in the individual shops of the cabinetworkers.

We must, perforce, draw sharp differences between provincial furniture and that made by Savery. Each was made within a few miles of the other and yet in each is reflected the intellectual conception of the maker and his patrons. The people living in outlying districts needed furniture to meet everyday demands, and because they lived the simplest of lives the simplest of furniture sufficed. As the frontiers pushed away to the westward, the contact with sophisticated city life was broken, and the small pioneer communities were thrown upon the skill of local cabinetworkers or the handy men of the homes.

Although we are aware of these facts it seems almost impossible to class the provincial furniture, with its crude, primitive charm, in the same period with the elegant refinement of Savery's creations. While he in Philadelphia was carving his splendid scrutoires, far out in the rural districts the

RURAL OPEN DRESSER OF WALNUT

native cabinetworker, feeling the urge for ornament upon his ill-shapen craftwork, painted gay designs in bright colors.

To be sure, William Savery did not at the start of his career produce the ornate pieces that we so closely associate with him. He began his trade in a simple way, favoring the severeness so loved by his own sect, the Quakers. His early furniture was of the simple type that we have already

RURAL PAINTED PINE DOWER CHEST

mentioned, and neither carved nor embellished. This may have been his own choice or it may have been done to meet the needs and desires of his thrifty clients.

The early years of Savery's life remain cloaked in mystery. In fact, it is only within the last twenty-five years that any information has been gleaned concerning him. We know that he was a Quaker and that he was born in 1722 and died in 1787. Like many of the prudent members of the Society of Friends, he early in life became a property owner and at the age of twenty-four was receiving an annual rental of fifty-two pounds, for a house on Third Street in Philadelphia. Public-spirited he seems to have been, for we find him serving as assessor in one of Philadelphia's city wards and later as collector of taxes for the guardians of the poor. His spirit,

EARLY SAVERY CHAIR WITH
SCROLLED SKIRT

which he so beautifully expressed in his work, may truly be said to represent that of the entire Philadelphia school of cabinetworkers. A few of the men who were working at this trade at the time of Savery were native-born, but we find that the majority of them came from England to open shop in this prosperous new-world city. Of this latter group one James Reynolds stands out conspicuously for his exquisite carving "in the newest and genteelest taste," as well as for his cabinetwork.

In undertaking a study of the work of William Savery, we must not neglect his early furniture in favor of that of the later period that has become so famed. There is an authentic chair which boasts a fiddle-back splat beautifully shaped and curved in a line with the back posts. The seat is rushed and edged with a narrow apron cut in rhythmic curves. The single front stretcher is of bulbous turnings and sets into the legs, which are of a simple Queen Anne cabriole type. Side stretchers are plain, as are the back posts. With simple dignified patterns of this type, Savery won the patronage of the Quakers.

Another early piece bearing the Savery label is a chest, with a slightly swelling, beautifully grained front face. The feet are molded, giving an accent of quiet refinement, and the handles, or "bales," as they are sometimes called, are plain and do not detract from the simplicity of the chest as a whole. This chest is important in our study, for it proves beyond doubt that Savery produced more than chairs in his humble outset as a cabinetmaker.

The label that has appeared on several pieces of his furniture unearthed in the last decade sheds little light on the breadth of his undertakings, for it bears only the legend, "William Savery, at the Sign of the Chair, near the market on Second Street." Savery used but the cheapest of printed labels throughout his work, though many of his competitors placed ornate copper-line engravings on their furniture, for an additional note of luxury.

TRIPOD TABLE

The first years of Savery's production dealt, as we have shown, with the simplest needs of a local patronage. A new stage began when, with the growth of his reputation, he increased his prices, immediately gaining a more wealthy clientele, which demanded an ornate and costlier style of furniture. Savery, rising to the occasion, put into play all of his hitherto hidden genius and created, for the everlasting fame of colonial cabinetworkers, the exquisitely carved and shaped pieces that have become famous throughout the land. By 1762, Chippendale's *The Gentleman and Cabinet-Maker's Director* was published, and from this volume Savery must have received much inspiration, for he worked in a Chippendale style that was never equaled by any other American craftsman. His furniture, however, was original enough

TEA TABLE WITH SHELL CARVING AND
ACANTHUS DECORATION

in construction and embellishment to warrant the designating of a "Savery school."

Good, honest workmanship went into every piece that he made, but without the foreign impetus that was given him he might have gone down in posterity as merely another good craftsman.

Philadelphia was becoming a wealthy city, and we find a highly cultured social life existing there as early as 1750. Fishing, shipbuilding, and trading with the West Indies in rum, molasses, sugar, and slaves brought a

SAVERY PIER TABLE WITH MARBLE TOP

tradesman class into the city, and with it, riches. Practically all of the dwellings were constructed of brick and boasted enormous flower gardens, which evoked much comment from visitors in the city. Music was given a prominent place in the home as well as in public life. An atmosphere of cultured reserve and liberal hospitality prevailed.

It is only natural that the consummate beauty of Savery's creations would flatter the vanity of this group of consumers, and we find that the Philadelphians were quickly won to the ornate Chippendale furniture.

There are extant examples from this school of nearly every known modern commodity of the furniture craft, although but a few of them can be attributed with authenticity to Savery. Nevertheless, they lead us to believe that his skilled hand created, aside from highboys, chairs, and

BROKEN ARCH HIGHBOY WITH FRAME
FINIALS AND TYPICAL SAVERY
DECORATION

SAVERY HIGHBOY WITH BUST AND
URN FINIALS

87

tables, such other pieces as desks, scrutoires, dressing tables, and bureaus. Two authentic dressing tables are in the George S. Palmer collection in the Metropolitan Museum in New York and are amongst the loveliest of the pieces that we know to be from the Savery shop. The aprons are elaborately carved and the center drawer displays the shell motif used so much upon his highboys.

A somewhat earlier dressing table, with a less elaborate shell, is in a Baltimore collection. On this piece pilasters are set in the recessed corners and a simple shell appears in the center of the apron. It is repeated upon the knees of the cabriole legs, as well as upon the center drawer, slightly elaborated. On this piece the drawer handles are wooden knobs, though most of Savery's furniture was graced with pierced brass pulls and escutcheons.

With this same formula Savery constructed his larger pieces, the scrutoires and high chests of drawers. In nearly every instance we may look for the shell or leafy scroll or both upon the center drawer of the lower part, the cabriole legs ornamented with shell or acanthus designs, broken arch pediments terminating in delicately wrought flowers, foliate scrolls elaborately carved and applied in the space between drawer tops and arch, end finials of urns and flames, and half-round fluted columns at the recessed corners of both the upper and lower sections.

An interesting variant is in the Metropolitan Museum in New York City. Here the pediment top is lighter in feeling and set upon a molded architrave consisting of a fillet, a cyma recta, two smaller fillets, a large fillet, and a dentil molding, above a two-inch molding carved with conventionalized flowers. An unusual touch appears in the finial, a carved wooden bust of a woman. This piece, although not known to have been made by Savery, is of Philadelphia manufacture and of the Savery school. The base contains, as in nearly all Savery pieces, one long drawer running the full width of the frame and three small drawers below. The top has three long drawers (sometimes, in other pieces, four) and a row of small drawers above. In some highboys of the Philadelphia school we find a row

BIRD CAGE TILT-TOP TABLE WITH PIE-CRUST TOP

of small drawers at the top of the upper carcass and above these, set into the space below the broken arch, a small rectangular or square drawer carved with the shell and scroll.

The smaller as well as the larger tripod tables boast the same elaborate leg as appears on the high chest, with an equally elaborate turned shaft. The round top displays a pie-crust or saucer edge sometimes broken at regular intervals with an acanthus motif and often fluted on the outer and lower edge.

Pier tables bore ornately carved aprons and the acanthus carvings of the legs were carried almost to the foot. Occasionally these tables, as well as the larger varieties, had black marble tops.

Savery's fame is equally warranted by his high chests and by his chairs. Most of the latter were of the side-chair variety, so called because they stood along the wall of a room. Nearly all of this type were made in sets of six or more. With all the elaborate carving, beautifully pierced splats, and graceful front legs of this style of chair, it seems difficult to realize that Savery used a primitive stump leg for the back, and we remain at a loss to account for it. Certainly cost would not have figured in it because for a few pennies more the leg could have been rounded and a club foot, such as we find on English chairs of this period, added. The only reason we can logically assign for this apparent crudity is that Savery, knowing that the chairs would stand most of the time against a wall, felt that their shortcomings would pass unobserved if the cabriole leg of the front was made beautiful enough to stand close inspection.

In 1760, an armchair appears with a graceful club foot at an unusual angle. The chair back was upholstered, as were the wings, which ran down into the arms and terminated in a scrolled wooden knuckle. The frame of the chair seat was carved in an elaborate apron with acanthus leaves and a human figure. The scrolled outline of the apron curved in an unbroken line into a cabriole leg with ball and claw foot. On the whole, Savery's furniture and that of his followers was fashioned unerringly in the Chippendale manner, and if for no other reason Savery and the Philadelphia school would have gained fame for their carving. Of a surprising degree of excellence, it may well be rated with that of Chippendale, and it strongly characterizes the individual style of this group of workers.

Some mention is due the many other cabinetworkers of Philadelphia of this same period. John Elliot, Jr., stands out predominant in the group and his work merits more than passing attention. He followed closely the styles of Chippendale and Savery. There are several pieces in existence that bear his label and as many others authentically attributed to him through bills of sale and old records.

Of Jonathan Gostelowe little is known at this date, but the attention of collectors has been called to his work by the recent unearthing of several

SAVERY CHAIR

interesting pieces. It is to be hoped that the future will disclose more. The baptismal font and communion table in Christ Church, Philadelphia, were made by him in 1788, and presented to the church, where they still remain in use. Only one piece of furniture has been found that bears his label, a small chest of drawers now owned by the Pennsylvania Museum.

Joseph and Stephen Armit, George Claypoole, Henry Clifton, and William Wayne may all be mentioned in connection with the Savery school. There were at the time in Philadelphia some twenty-seven recognized master craftsmen and, from what we may gather when actual furniture specimens are missing, all were working in the Savery manner. From the above-mentioned shops we have known pieces of work, and in every case they retain the characteristics of construction and detail that mark the Philadelphia furniture of the era.

It is only right that we give some attention at this point to a man not professionally associated with the furniture industry but who left a marked effect on many of the cabinetworkers and carvers of the day. Samuel McIntire was born and died in Salem, Massachusetts, and followed the architect's profession, although it is doubtful that he ever had any actual training in such lines. His best work is still to be seen in many of the doorways, mantels, and other woodwork features of old Salem homes. His father, a joiner by trade, no doubt gave Samuel his early training but we find him shortly turning to woodcarving and home designing, and an announcement of his death in a Salem paper in 1811 declares his occupation to have been that of a housewright. The houses that he built bear no particular display of genius as an architect, but their embellishments, window frames, cornices, mantels, doors, and gateposts are exquisitely designed and carved. At various times during his life, McIntire made small medallions, busts, and other carved and finished ornaments which he sold to cabinetworkers for use on furniture. Some of these ornaments we are led to believe found their way into the hands of the Philadelphia cabinetworkers of whom we have just spoken. A very few center bust finials on highboys and small appliquéd ornaments on other furniture bear enough resemblance in subject matter and detail to his work to warrant our classing them as such. We shall probably never know, if this is true, by what route they came into the Philadelphia shops, unless we may presume that the furniture makers of this city realized that in McIntire they had the artistic descendant of Adam and Wren.

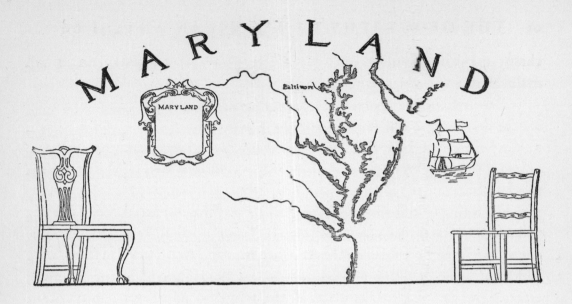

CHAPTER V

CHIPPENDALE, SHERATON, AND HEPPLEWHITE[1]

THE end of the Seventeenth Century marked the opening of a new era for all Europe and America. We may give this as an approximate date of the beginning of modern history. The period of discovery and colonization was over. The boundaries of the known world had been greatly extended and many new channels of trade had been opened. Ships of every nation were plying the seas, and there resulted an expansion of trade and economic prosperity. Broader contacts made possible by the age of discovery, and the intellectual stimulus of the Renaissance resulted in a broader life with more complex social and cultural elements.

It is only natural that in all the departments of daily life America should look upon England as a criterion. Regular, steady trade between her ports and those of England kept her in constant touch with the life of the mother country and brought travelers from one land to the other. New England and the middle colonies were concentrating their energies

---

[1] To Maryland I have assigned the three great Georgian craftsmen, for she, possibly more than any other of the thirteen original states, has retained and glorified the Georgian traditions.

chiefly upon shipbuilding and trade. Agriculture was carried on on a small scale to satisfy local needs. Busy seaports along the entire Atlantic coast were becoming social centers and shortly centers of wealth and population. In the South, agriculture was carried on with a flourish and tobacco, rice, and other food crops formed the basis of a growing local and foreign trade and laid the foundation for the great wealth that later extended throughout the South.

With the establishment of a complete and well-ordered social life the utilitarian arts came into prominence. Trade with hitherto inaccessible countries brought exotic influences into Europe and America that were shortly destined to play a great part in the development of the furniture crafts. The easy and affluent life of the larger social centers, in constant touch with European culture, came to rival that of the mother country, and drew aristocratic travelers to these shores.

The development of local arts and crafts received whole-hearted support and in 1733 the Society of the Dilettanti was organized with no other purpose than to patronize and encourage the arts.

In all, the period was marked by an intellectual and spiritual quickening, economic prosperity, and a concurrent patronage of the arts in both public and home life. Foreign influences from Europe and the Orient were preparing for the eclectic taste which characterizes the century.

These years from 1700 to 1730 we may term transitional and preparatory to the Georgian era, which begins in the late part of the second quarter of the century. During the reign of Queen Anne some of the heavier Jacobean lines in architecture and furniture had been replaced, but French and Dutch influences remained predominant throughout her reign. With the ascension of George I to the throne of England in 1740 a marked change appears in all phases of designing and an era ensues which we may justly call the most refined through which architecture and the furniture crafts have passed.

Chippendale's name stands first in the line of Eighteenth Century

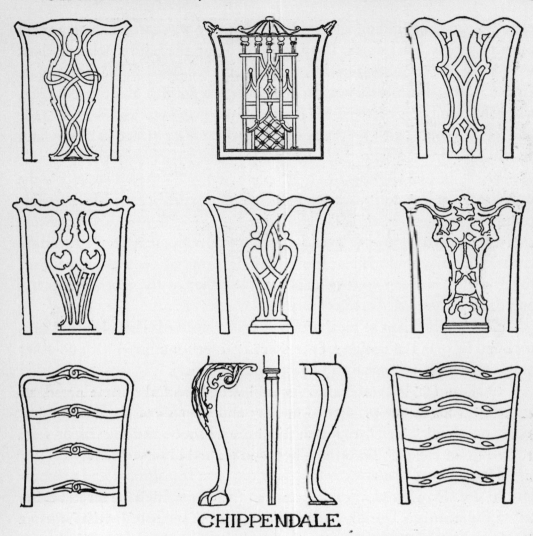

CHIPPENDALE

CHARACTERISTIC CHAIR BACKS AND LEGS

designers that ended with Sheraton and included in its ranks Hepplewhite, the brothers Adam, Manwaring, Ince and Mayhew, Wedgewood, Angelica Kaufmann, and Shearer. A short résumé of the works of Chippendale, Sheraton, and Hepplewhite is essential to an understanding of the influence which their styles exerted in this country.

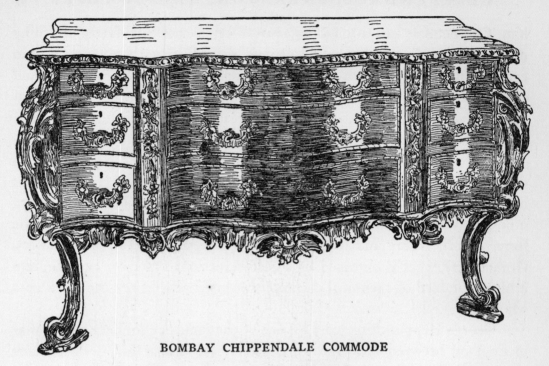

BOMBAY CHIPPENDALE COMMODE

Thomas Chippendale, son of a cabinetmaker of the same name, accompanied his father to London in 1727 and soon showed unusual talent as a carver and joiner. In his first furniture he shows little deviation from the accepted style of Queen Anne but soon we find him producing furniture after the style of Louis XV.

The year 1740 marks the beginning of Chippendale's career as arbiter of English furniture patterns and also marks the decline of Dutch influence in England and the discarding of walnut for mahogany. In this respect Chippendale has long been known as "the high priest of mahogany."

Passing successively through periods strongly influenced by the French rococo of Louis XV, then by Chinese and Gothic, and finally by classic and Louis XVI, we find his best work produced between the years 1750 and 1760. Not permitting himself to be handicapped by technical problems, seizing inspiration from everything that had been created before him, Chippendale ran through a gamut of styles, not originating anything distinctly new but rather adapting and embellishing that which was in common use. Blessed with a fertile imagination and a facile hand, as well as the goodwill and patronage of England's most influential families, including the Court, he created a body of work more elegant and an influence more widespread than did any man before him.

Chippendale's greatest innovation was the cutting out in an openwork design of the solid chair splat so favored in the Queen Anne styles. To this he gives a light and varied treatment and tops it with his second great innovation, the cupid's bow cresting. Square seats replace the horseshoe form of earlier date and counterbalance the lightness of other members. Ornamental effect is obtained by varied structural shapes or carving, and a high standard of technical accomplishment characterizes the work as a whole.

George Hepplewhite, least known of the famous trio, became popular in England between 1765 and 1775. He is best known for his shield-back chairs and the beauty and simplicity of his ornament, which included the wheat-ear, the honeysuckle, and the three plumes of the Prince of Wales. A particularly charming detail that appears on many of his pieces is the small rosette in a panel corner and the rounding of the panel about the motif.

Thomas Sheraton, last and greatest, from an artistic point of view, of the Georgians, left in addition to his furniture a book on the subject, *The Cabinetmaker and Upholsterer's Drawing Book*, as famous as his name and rivaled only by Chippendale's *The Gentleman and Cabinet-Maker's Director*. His best period remains unsurpassed for delicacy, grace of proportion, and restraint. Carving was to Sheraton merely an additional embellishment to be applied when form and color had reached perfection and never to be used to conceal structural error or weakness. Though less versatile than Chippendale, Sheraton as an artist and inventor far surpassed him. Particularly characteristic is his use of inlay, his intricate chair backs, and the ef-

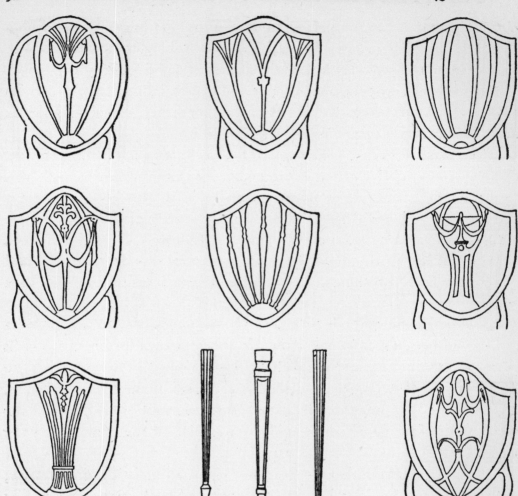

HEPPLEWHITE

CHARACTERISTIC CHAIR BACKS AND LEGS

fects that he obtained by dyeing "harewood," a sycamore cut, and using it in combination with woods of other tones and grains.

So much for these designers. An understanding of the styles which they created in England will furnish a working basis for the study of American interpretations, but before proceeding let us look into the causes which

SHERATON

CHARACTERISTIC CHAIR BACKS AND LEGS

led to the acceptance of these styles to the exclusion of everything else for a period of twenty-five years.

We have shown earlier in the chapter the general causes of the wave of prosperity that was sweeping over the American colonies. Throughout the first half of the Eighteenth Century these influences had been at work

CHIPPENDALE CHAIR SHOWING
CHINESE INFLUENCE

slowly changing the daily life and manner of living. The development of a highly organized society was in progress and this development was based upon both aristocracy and wealth. When, thirty years prior to the Revolution, Chippendale's furniture was introduced from England, the craze spread like wildfire over the whole country. The elegance and ornateness of this type satisfied the desires of the affluent for a more showy style of furnishing, and within two or three years every cabinetmaker in this country seems to have turned his hand to reproducing the designs of Thomas

CHIPPENDALE CHAIR SHOWING ROCOCO
INFLUENCE

Chippendale. The wealthier colonists, not wishing to risk locally made pieces, sent to England for originals and although unfortunately we cannot trace them with any degree of authenticity, we know that some of Chippendale's work made its way into this country. Silks, damasks, leather, and turkey work were imported for upholstery and large firms came into existence whose sole business was the procuring and selling of these fabrics.

We are more interested in the work of American cabinetmakers who

CHIPPENDALE BOOKCASE

fell under the spell of Chippendale than we are in the great master himself, and it is well to pause here and consider the differences, either structural or ornamental, that mark their works. Chippendale's book on cabinetwork was first published in 1753 and shortly afterward found its way into the hands of our joiners and carvers. Knowing this, we may expect exact duplicates of designs which appear in the volume. Occasionally we find them, but the manner of execution was not the same and more often we find a characteristic interpretation which distinguishes the American pieces from mere copies.

CHIPPENDALE SERPENTINE-FRONT CHEST OF DRAWERS WITH
DWARFED CABRIOLE LEGS

We have shown in the chapter on Savery how this cabinetworker more perhaps than any other expressed the spirit of Chippendale furniture. But there were many others who utilized their own technical skill in producing for their local trade furniture that would take the place of imported pieces and still have the outstanding qualities that made the latter pieces desirable.

It is to be expected that many of the details of construction would be identical with those that preceded, for they had been proven satisfactory and no change was necessary. Among these, we still find the seat rails mor-

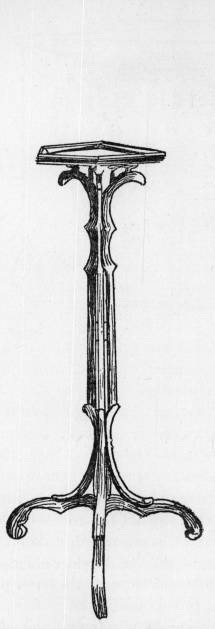

CHIPPENDALE CANDLE-
STAND

CHIPPENDALE FIRE SCREEN

104

CHIPPENDALE DOG-FOOT TABLE

tised through the back legs and the tenons showing clearly at the rear. The splats were treated in a true Chippendale manner, with interlacing ribbons, Gothic or Chinese fretwork, and typical carvings of the acanthus, cords, ribbons, and bowknots. The Chinese and Gothic taste never became widely popular in this country, although there remain a few examples of the style that we may attribute to local cabinetworkers. The edges of seat rails are cut in ornate shapes, or cut plain with a bead molding about the upper and lower edges. The cabriole foot was carved at the knee and often a distance down the leg. The ball and claw foot is realistically carved and almost without fail appears on every cabriole leg of this period. Top rails of chairs are bow-shaped and end in slightly straightened ears, or rosette forms.

The highboy, chest-on-chest, and chest of drawers occupy a prominent position in the home furnishings of the period. They boast cabriole legs, scrolled pediment tops, carved aprons and drawer fronts, and ornate brasses. A few more conservative pieces exist, with architectural moldings and restrained carving, that are essentially more lovely than the ornate

CHIPPENDALE BROKEN ARCH
SECRETARY WITH GLAZED
GOTHIC DOORS

examples and seem without exception to have had their origin in New England. Lowboys correspond in all detail with the highboys.

One of the most exquisite pieces of furniture at this time was the chest of drawers. On these pieces we find bracket feet of delicate proportion, or dwarfed cabrioles, and above the feet at the base of the carcass, a narrow

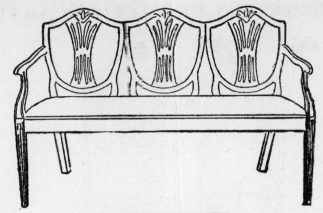

A.—HEPPLEWHITE

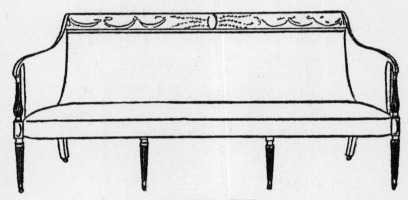

B.—SHERATON

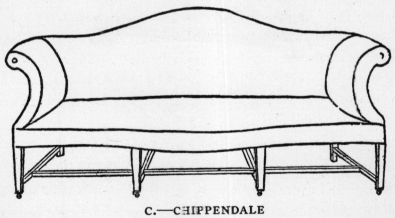

C.—CHIPPENDALE

CHARACTERISTIC SOFAS

107

CHIPPENDALE ARMCHAIR

molding. Carefully selected wood for drawer fronts gives these chests an additional beauty. The corners are finished with a quarter column and about the drawers we often find a tiny molding. Brasses again were of the ornate willow pattern. A very few chests had the *bombé* or swollen front with ornate acanthus carvings carried up the carcass from the short legs, to accent the outward curved line of the cabinet. The drawers of these pieces follow the line of the curve.

Tables appear in an endless variety, tripod, tip-tops, pier, drop-leaf, and dining. On these we find the same details of construction and ornament that mark the other pieces. Cabriole legs are used on the long dining tables and pier tables, as well as on some of the other large varieties.

Smaller tables with center shaft have the cabriole legs and a turned

CHIPPENDALE TEA TABLE

CHIPPENDALE PIER TABLE

SHERATON BUTLER'S DESK WITH
GLAZED DOORS

shaft running from the platform above. In the so-called bird-cage type a
secondary platform appears at the top of the shaft with four small uprights to hold the weight of the top. Small rectangular pier tables have
cabriole legs and carved aprons, and in many cases marble tops and small
brass railings.

SHERATON SECRETARY

III

SHERATON SIDEBOARD

Desks are of the slant-top variety with drawers below, and bracket feet, or raised off the floor on long cabriole legs. There are also the knee-hole and secretary types. In the latter style the top had either glazed or wooden doors. The small desk supported on four legs and the knee-hole desk were never in common use in this country despite the fact that both are practical, serviceable pieces of furniture and lack the bulk of the larger pieces.

Sofas of the Chippendale style were also uncommon in this country, although a few splendid pieces are known. One of these displays the usual somewhat shortened cabriole leg with carved and shaped skirt and another in the author's collection has straight tapered legs with recessed stretcher. The arms of all these sofas are outswelling and upholstered, as are the back and seat. The upholstery of the seat is carried over the front rail while in the sides and back the same method is used.

HEPPLEWHITE DINING TABLE

Clocks of the period are usually tall, and ornamented far beyond those of the preceding style. Small quarter-round columns finish the sides of the cases and flank the arched doors of the face. A broken pediment forms the cresting, with corner urn and central finials of brass or wood and often fretwork in the opening of the arch. Carving is more restrained on clocks than on any other Chippendale furniture, and their greatest beauty is in the wood that was used in the cases.

The mahogany used in American furniture of this period was of the Santo Domingo variety and is noteworthy for the beauty of its grain and color. Veneers were made of the crotch or burl cuts and practically no inlay appears throughout the style.

The vogue for Chippendale furniture passed with the beginning of the Revolution and the breaking of close affiliations with the mother country, a drawing apart caused not only by war, but also by wider trade and travel

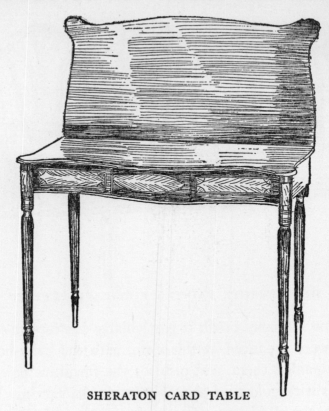

SHERATON CARD TABLE

on the part of Americans. The years of the Revolution were trying ones for the country, and little attention was given the decorative arts. At the close of the war independence brought in its wake an increased trade and local manufacture, which England had restricted when the colonies were under her dominion. At the time of the French Revolution large groups of immigrants, drawn mostly from the nobility and cultured classes, brought into the United States the French classicism that was at the same time influencing the work of English cabinetmakers, more particularly Sheraton and Hepplewhite. It is not surprising to find these styles being copied over here, despite the evident distaste for all that was English. It is rather to be regretted that the French Empire influence followed so closely upon that of Sheraton and to a marked extent decreased its duration in this country.

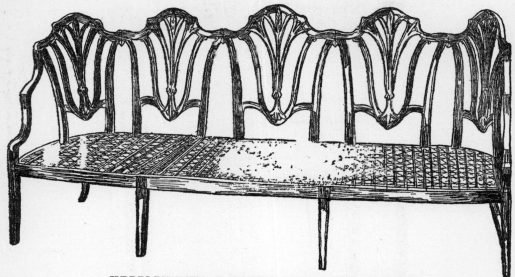

HEPPLEWHITE PAINTED FIVE-BACK SETTEE

To Sheraton influence credit is particularly due for the splendid side-boards which were produced at this time, with the knife-boxes that invariably accompanied them, and also for the furniture painted in grays and pale greens with gold used as an accent on the carving. Proportion is light and delicate in all Sheraton furniture, and the use of carefully chosen veneer and inlay heightens the effect of slenderness and grace. Carving is used to a great extent on the variously shaped splats of chairs, and turnings are so slender as to appear weak. Window seats and wing chairs are common and retain the delicacy of the side chairs. Sofas consist of three, four, or five carved wooden chair backs, or are upholstered similarly to those of Chippendale. Chests of drawers are small and the fronts are curved or serpentine. Inlay of satin-wood and fruit woods appears around drawer fronts and key-plates. The slant-top desk remains about the same as in the earlier period but now the French foot is made of a solid piece with the sides and front and the line is unbroken by a bottom molding. Inlay is used on the desks in a fashion similar to the chests of drawers and particular attention is given the decorative effects on the lid. Secretary desks have

HEPPLEWHITE SIDEBOARD

broken arch crestings with a marked lack of carving and a sufficient architectural quality to make them truly expressive of the period. In many of these secretaries the desk equipment appears in a drawer with drop front rather than in the typical slant-top style. These desks are often and without any apparent reason called "butlers' desks." In still another type the desk equipment is hidden behind tambour work. This consisted of small strips of wood glued upon a canvas back in such a way that the pliable quality of cloth was given an otherwise seemingly wooden panel.

Dining tables were made in three or more sections. These sections could be used in two parts, end to end, or all together to make a table that was often fifteen feet in length. The legs of these tables retain the delicacy found in those of the chairs, and the tops, of carefully selected and matched mahogany, were sometimes ornamented with delicate bands of contrasting inlay. The aprons were narrow and they, too, were inlaid with bands or patterns of lighter woods. The table top was rectangular, but in most cases the end pieces were rounded. All in all, these tables have come down to us unimproved both in beauty of design and in practicality.

Card tables are usually rounded and beautifully ornamented with characteristic inlay. They have one leaf which rests against the wall in console fashion when the table is not in use. Some of these leaves are held up by a fourth leg which folds against the back when not in use.

Sideboards are long and narrow and have either four or six legs. In a few instances the fronts are serpentine in shape and built about a center arched opening. Other pieces show one or two long drawers at the top of the carcass with doors at either end below and a deep drawer in the center. The panel forms are round, oval, and rectangular, and characteristically inlaid. Wherever possible some detail of inlaid ornament appears on the fronts of these pieces. Nothing but the highest praise can be given these sideboards, which are now being sought after by those collectors who

SHERATON
KNIFE-BOX

CHIPPENDALE
KNIFE-BOX

CHIPPENDALE WING CHAIR

demand in their furniture finished cabinetry as well as sophistication of line.

We shall follow in the next chapter the influence of Sheraton and Hepplewhite on a New York designer, Duncan Phyfe, and trace these influences through to the debased pieces that we find in the late Empire style.

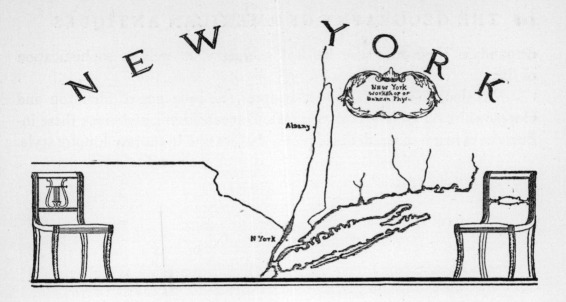

CHAPTER VI

DUNCAN PHYFE AND LATE EMPIRE

AT THE close of the Revolution a feeling of cordial dislike for anything British and an equally strong admiration for anything French prevailed throughout the United States. As a result every element of daily life, architecture, furniture, and even clothing aped the French neoclassicism. Out of the untimely and ill-befitting interpretations that followed rose a master craftsman; one who redeemed Empire furniture in this country and saved it, if only for a few years, from the degradation into which it was destined to sink—Duncan Phyfe. In the afterglow of Sheraton the spark of his genius flared up brightly for a while before it, too, was dimmed with the rest.

Phyfe, a Scotchman by birth, came to this country with his family in 1784 at the age of sixteen and settled near Albany. In that city he served his apprenticeship and later opened his first shop. Eventually the wealth of New York, already a growing metropolis, attracted him, for we find him established in Partition Street (later Fulton Street) in 1795. Prior to this, he seems to have conducted a business in Broad Street and we know that he encountered many difficulties there before fortune brought his work to the attention of the John Jacob Astor family. Through their patronage, he eventually established a wealthy clientele.

As Phyfe reached the heyday of his creative life he could look back upon the great English designers of the Georgian school as a group and profit by their innovations and errors, and it is only logical to find that between the years 1795 and 1818 nearly all the furniture that he made bore characteristics of these men, particularly of Sheraton.

From 1818 to 1830, the best of all American Empire furniture came out of his shop. Original enough to warrant a separate classification, it lacked the bulk and artificiality of the Napoleonic pieces and retained all the grace and delicate charm of Sheraton. Line and proportion were excellent, carving and ornament were used with restraint, and all workmanship was unexcelled.

From 1830 until his retirement in 1847, Phyfe unfortunately fell under the wave of degenerate, overcarved rosewood furniture which persisted in America until the opening years of the Twentieth Century. None of the articles made during this period show any of his former excellence and we shall pass them by as the unfortunate effects of fad upon a cabinetworker of genius.

In 1837 Phyfe took his sons into the partnership and the firm name becomes "Duncan Phyfe and Sons." In 1840 it is "Duncan Phyfe and Son" and remains so until he sells out the business in 1847, to retire. He died in New York City in 1854, having lived a quiet, unpretentious life, mingling rarely with his fellow men except when business demanded. He is known to have made an exquisite box in which bottles of water from Lake Erie were sent to Lafayette as a souvenir of the opening of the Erie Canal but aside from this we can find no record of public notice accorded him as an important figure in the business life of the city.

The social life in New York at the opening of the Nineteenth Century was sophisticated and elegant. The city was enjoying a period of great wealth and prosperity. Public taste was not at a high tide of excellence, and was easily swayed by fad. Fortunately for Phyfe, at this time his reputation had spread even to neighboring cities and orders poured in from the wealthier residents of New York, Boston, and Philadelphia. Needless to state, as Phyfe's reputation grew and an excellent patronage was assured him his prices were adequately increased. In fact, these prices correspond almost identically with prices of well-made furniture to-day. We can judge well the extent to which his business had grown by the fact that he now occupied 33, 34, and 35 Fulton Street and had in his employ more than a hundred cabinetworkers and carvers.

The distinguished character of Phyfe's furniture resulted from his remarkable ability to combine the best elements of the Georgian designers with the severe simplicity of the post-Revolution furniture of France without sacrificing one to the other. In accomplishing this he retained his own originality of design and excellence of execution, and these qualities lifted him from the rank of an everyday craftsman to the height of his profession.

It is safe to say that more pieces of authenticated Phyfe furniture exist than of any other American designer, and although not all of them were actually made by his hand, nevertheless we feel sufficiently that his personality permeates them all. His fame we may justly attribute to his conceptions as a whole or to his restrained use of exquisite ornament, whether carving or veneer. In Phyfe's case veneer, although we may not observe it at first glance, was one of his chief elements in obtaining certain decorative effects. In general, all of his pieces are rectangular in shape, but less bulky and cumbersome than the prevailing continental mode.

Chairs and tables are probably the most representative pieces of Phyfe furniture although it goes on record that sofas, beds, sideboards, and bureaus were made in the Fulton Street shop, no doubt on special order to match chairs and tables. In the earliest of these pieces it is not unusual to find plain turned legs although the leg that we recognize as distinctly

PHYFE DROP-LEAF TABLE

characterizing Phyfe furniture was concave, ending in a brass lion's foot or carved wooden dog's paw, and ornamented at the knee with acanthus carving.

In general structure and style Phyfe's chairs are all similar, but in decorative detail they vary greatly. The front legs are curved forward and the back legs swing in a backward curved line from the top rail to the floor. Arms also begin at the top rail and run in deep curves to the arm support, which is scrolled, carved, or turned in an urn shape.

PHYFE CONSOLE TAELE

In the side chair we find a single line carried from the top rail into the line of the seat and often continuous down the front leg to the floor. Arms, the front of the back posts, front legs, and seat rails are reeded or carved with the acanthus. The broad panel of the back displays carved oak branches, wheat-ears, thunderbolts, or cornucopias. Backs have a lyre splat, some form of the curved cross-rail, or solid, shaped horizontal panels.

These elements we find more or less combined in all Phyfe's chairs. Front legs may be round and carved and back legs square, and in many cases the front legs are straight and the back curved. No definite rule seems to have been applied to such constructions, although because the front legs alone were carved we find that their forms vary greatly, as those of the back legs do not.

A chair fashioned after the curule seats of Rome was made in Phyfe's

PHYFE SINGLE AND DOUBLE CROSS-RAIL CHAIRS

shop, and is typical of the French Empire influence. The legs consist of double reverse curves crossed in the center and ending in brass lion's feet. Of this style two distinctly different examples exist. In one the back legs are identical with those found in the cross-rail chair and at the front the curved curule legs appear. The other has the curved legs at either side connected by a center stretcher. At the crossing of the curved legs appears a small carved medallion.

Some of the chairs made by this craftsman have caned seats but most of them are upholstered over frames which set themselves into the seat rail. In still others, and in many of the sofas, the upholstering is put directly

PHYFE WINDOW SEAT

PHYFE LYRE-BACK CHAIR

on to the seat rails. On a few sofas the front rail is concealed by the upholstery.

Cross-bars appear both doubly and singly as well as curved and straight. A small rosette is placed where they cross and almost without exception we find that they are reeded. The shaped horizontal splats consist of a small medallion or rectangle, uncarved and supported by carved scrolls. In a few of these splats the medallion is veneered. The lyre, as it appears in chair backs, sofa backs and arms, and table supports is carved of wood, beautifully decorated with the acanthus. The strings, either four or five in number, are of brass or whalebone and the pin which runs through

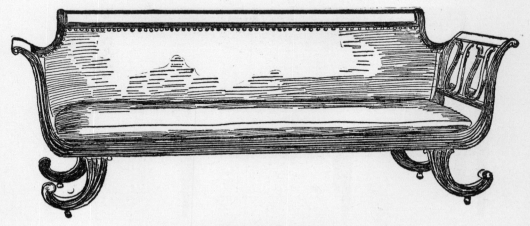

PHYFE LYRE SOFA

the top is of ebony. When the lyre appears on tables it is, perforce, heavier
and less delicately carved. Reeding appears on practically all Phyfe furniture.
The front face of the back supports,
often the top of the seat rail, particularly when it is continuous with the
back line, and the front legs all are
reeded in nearly every case. Occasionally the front legs are carved with the
acanthus or the dog foot which reaches
half or more of the way up the leg to
join abruptly the more conventional
upper member.

The acanthus appears on the lyre in
combination with parallel reeding, and
on the front legs in some instances. Unlike his predecessors', Phyfe's acanthus
consists merely of a series of grooves

PHYFE CARVED RAIL DOG-FOOT
CHAIR

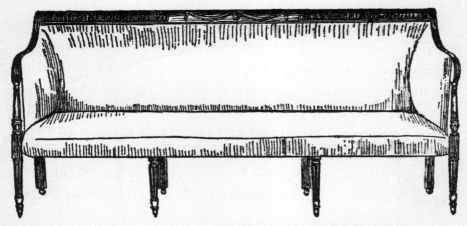

PHYFE SOFA WITH SHERATON INFLUENCE

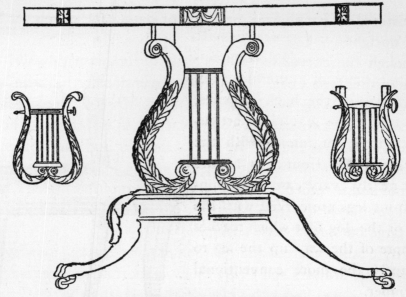

CHARACTERISTIC DETAILS OF PHYFE LYRES

and ridges extending from a long center ridge which runs the entire length of the leaf.

Armchairs and sofas to correspond with all types of chairs were made in Phyfe's workshop and a few footstools exist which warrant the belief that they, too, were made to complete sets of drawing-room furniture. The most usual from his shop, found so far, shows strong Sheraton influence with straight tapering legs and a predominant feeling of straight lines in their construction. The top rails are usually paneled in three or four rectangles, each or one of which is carved. The reeded arms curve from the top rail in an outward swing and end in a small scroll which rests upon a baluster with reeded shaft and carved urn. Front and side rails display parallel reeding unless as in some cases the former is covered by the upholstery. Nearly all of these sofas

CHARACTERISTIC PHYFE BEDPOSTS

are upholstered on back, arms, and seat or have cane panels set between rails and uprights.

Although the curved-leg Phyfe chair is comparatively well known, few sofas of this type exist. There is one exceptionally beautiful example in the American Wing of the Metropolitan Museum, New York City. This piece displays two exquisite lyre splats set in either arm. The top rail of the back as well as that of the arm is straight and they are connected with a small wooden curve. The armpost sweeps in a continuous line into the seat rail and is reeded. Another sofa of this type has paneled rails, and lion's feet terminate the legs, which are carved ornately and join the seat rail in a large outspread eagle's wing.

Of Phyfe tables there is an overwhelming variety: the four-legged type with or without drawers and shelf; those supported on a center pedestal, such as a lyre or urn; and a third type fashioned after the trestle table and supported at either end by a lyre or coupled *colonnettes*. A few card tables of Phyfe origin exist with the fifth leg swinging out at one side to hold the extended leaf. These tables show strongly the Sheraton influence, which characterizes the four-legged variety, and fall under that category.

In this first general style of table Phyfe employed with great delicacy the best details of the Sheraton period. Tapering reeded legs end in characteristically turned small members. The legs above the turned portion are reeded and run up into a long block into which the skirting is set. Tops are square or rectangular, with oval, scalloped, or Pembroke corners. Drop leaves are occasionally used at either side or singly in the back as in the case of the card table. Sometimes the skirting is plain, and at other times paneled. In a few examples a small rectangular panel appears on one side only and is carved with drapery swag or leaves. The top block of the leg often displays minute inlaid rectangles with square or oval tops. This particular inlay seems to have been representative of the exquisite detail Phyfe put in all his work.

With the addition of two small drawers or one large drawer or both,

PHYFE GAME TABLE

and a shaped shelf set between the legs just above the feet, we have the Phyfe serving table. On this table the corners of the case are set into a fluted three-quarter column which is a continuation of the leg. The top curves out over the leg at each corner.

The second type of table, so beautiful from the hands of Phyfe and so enormously bad from the hands of his less gifted imitators, consists of a small platform upheld by three or four concave legs and supporting above it a center shaft of a single turned column or the lyre, as the case may be. The single shaft usually consisted of an urn, carved with the acanthus or reeded, and above it, supporting the top, a reeded or turned column. The concave legs bore the acanthus or reeding or both, and the platform, rectangular or round in shape, was also reeded at the sides. A brass lion's foot

PHYFE DROP-LEAF TABLE SHOWING SHERATON INFLUENCE

terminates each leg. In the case of the lyre shaft the platform is always square or rectangular. The lyre is carved with the acanthus or reeded, and in general follows the construction of the lyre that was used in chair backs.

A console card table with a center shaft has an unusual inner mechanism that when the leaf is lowered automatically throws the third concave leg out to form a perfect tripod. A very few tables of this same period have center shafts composed of coupled colonnettes which we shall describe in detail later.

Both of these types appear in the extension drop-leaf dining tables and in similar dining tables of smaller dimensions, while the third and last type is confined almost entirely to library and dressing tables.

In this group, coupled colonnettes or the lyre are supported on rectan-

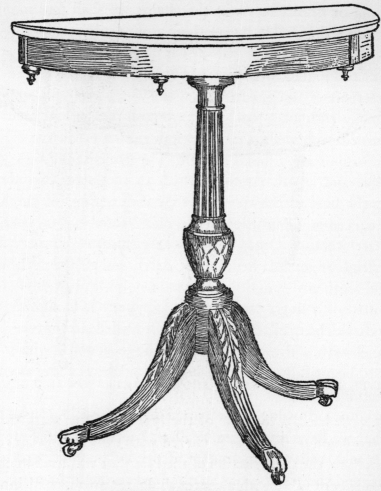

PHYFE CONSOLE TABLE

gular platforms at either end of the table. From two sides of the platform
extend concave legs. Usually one or more drawers are set into the skirt and
a delicately shaped stretcher or small shelf runs between the platforms.
The colonnettes are light and beautifully turned while shelf and table edge
are reeded or carved. Corner blocks often end in small finials or have small
rectangles of inlay in decorative patterns set on each of the outer faces.
Occasionally within a small paneled rectangle on the skirt is carved a

drapery swag or branches. As in the chairs, we shall find many variants in Phyfe's tables that fall in two of these groups rather than consistently in one.

Beds of the four-post variety are attributed to Phyfe and in general are characteristic of those of Sheraton and Hepplewhite. Usually they are high and made without a footboard and with a very low headboard. The feet are turned and run up into a rectangular block from which rises a carved urn supporting a fluted column. The urn is sometimes carved with the acanthus and at other times reeded. In the latter case the acanthus appears at the base of the column below the reeding. At the head of the column is carved an adaptation of the palm-leafed capital that we find in Egyptian architecture. Other decorations include the drapery and wheat-ears. The sleigh or gondola bed appears later, and although the curved line of head and footboards might lead us to term it Duncan Phyfe in style, we can attribute not a single example of this type to his manufacture.

A Phyfe sideboard is extant with thin reeded and carved legs, center arched panel with a drawer above, and large doors at either side. This piece boasts beautifully veneered borders on drawer and door fronts as well as around the top.

Piano stands, dressing glasses, and buffets follow in general the characteristics that we have attributed to Phyfe, but all of these are rare.

Phyfe, as no other cabinetmaker, depended upon his wood for decorative effects, and the results that he obtained through the use of veneer are unique in the annals of American cabinetwork. Minute borders around corner blocks of tables, and wider borders about drawer fronts, at the lower edge of skirtings, and along the sides of table tops all are characteristic of the care which Phyfe exercised in making the minutest detail beautiful. All of the veneer was made of carefully selected woods, usually crotch or curly mahogany, and by matching, juxtaposing, or contrasting the grain of the separate pieces he procured remarkable decorative effects on small and large surfaces. In his carved ornamentation Phyfe also excelled. The demand for fine materials was a result of the increasing wealth of the city and the growth of a complicated system of social life, with attendant cultural elements. Phyfe interpreted this affluence in his furniture with a cautious restraint that ever kept within the bounds of refined taste. The European elements, first British and later French as the vogue demanded, appear in his work but never overcome his refined taste. To him we may credit the fact that American Empire furniture at this time far excelled that of both France and England and for many years stayed far above the banal and ugly monstrosities into which the European styles fell but a few years after their inception. Carving as used by this master craftsman is always low in relief and unaffected in its simplicity, and next to his use of veneer may be said to be the most characteristic element of Phyfe's work.

Until 1830 Duncan Phyfe stayed the wave of garishness, but at that time he succumbed along with the rest, and there ensued a period that we shall designate as Late Empire. This period lasts but a short while, then becomes lost in the Victorian era. At times, of course, in the great quantity of furniture produced (never were homes more over-furnished) we are bound to find a flare of grace and beauty, but on the whole the period was marked with banality and artificiality.

Furniture assumed monstrous size, with pompous and vulgar carving and no grace of line to redeem its enormousness. What few Sheraton details remain are so magnified as to become hideous. All ornament is cumbersome and brutal. In fact, little can be said for the period aside from the fact that workmanship still remained of the best.

Napoleon in his spectacular career was the only

CHARACTERISTIC
EARLY EMPIRE CHAIR

individual who ever dictated a period style and saw it carried out. The success of this unnatural style for a while may be attributed only to the fact that Napoelon had at his command a group of the greatest and most talented craftsmen and artists then living. Any furniture style not a direct outgrowth of the sentiments, aspirations, and lives of the populace at large is at its incipience false and destined to a rapid death. With the passing of a few short years, decadent tendencies creep into the French furniture and American craftsmen, depending still upon foreign inspiration, do little else than magnify these undesirable qualities. Not all the blame for what followed may be laid to France, for taste throughout our country was at low ebb and the work of conservative designers was not acceptable to the people. And, too, water power, which had been the mainstay of local cabinetworkers, was replaced by steam, and machines were invented which did the work of many carvers and turners in a fraction of the time that was formerly required, and quantity production ruined quality. The clipper-ship period saw the building of our merchant marine and the opening of a great market for furniture that had not existed before. Manufactories established in New England could depend upon far-distant as well as local consumption and the output was automatically increased to meet these demands. Hand-cut veneer became replaced with thicker machine cuts and the chief beauty of this decorative method was lost. The pendulum had swung, but unfortunately too far, and nearly a century was required to rid the country of the miscreated results.

In actual furniture pieces it is a simple matter to trace the elegant qualities of Phyfe and Sheraton to their decadent

EARLY EMPIRE SEWING TABLE

EARLY EMPIRE CONSOLE TABLE WITH
CARVED PEDESTAL

stage. Sideboards probably show more clearly than any other pieces the results of enlarging and over-carving. The fronts remain severely straight or curve slightly and contain three or more drawers with cupboards below. This construction automatically brings the carcass of the piece nearer the floor and the slender legs of the earlier examples are replaced with massive,

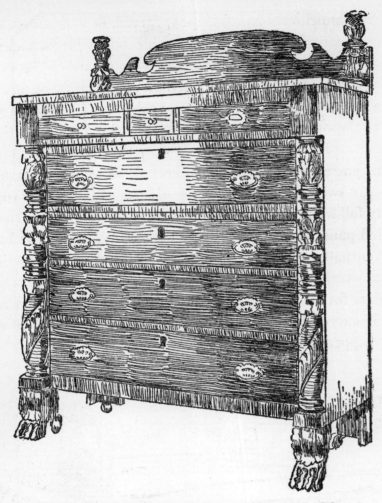

EMPIRE BUREAU WITH CARVED PILLARS

round, carved, or twisted pillars, terminating in a lion's or bear's foot realistically carved. The piece has become massive in general appearance and when slight ornament is applied, as in some cases, its beauty is overwhelmed by the bulk of the carcass.

Curves, wherever they appear, are too broken by carving to carry as continuous, graceful lines. This is particularly noticeable in table construction. We find clumsy bases, turned, carved, or gadrooned, with exaggerated thick concave legs. The pineapple and acanthus carvings are placed, not too sparingly, upon the center support, which rests on plinths, supported by carved ball-and-claw feet. In a few cases we are bound to recognize a certain dignity in this type of table but more often we are too conscious of the over-ambitious carver to perceive what beauties may lie hidden.

As time passes, every surface is veneered: on sofas, chairs, and tables. Bureaus sport swollen curves at either side, with the small top drawers occasionally following the line of the curve but more often recessed behind it. A scrolled panel or straight piece of wood is placed at the back of the top and eventually small drawers are added to this construction. Enormous round wooden or glass knobs serve as pulls. Dwarfed, carved, and twisted pillars form the legs and at the ends of the carcass we sometimes find ornately carved thick columns breaking the corners. At the same time this feature appears on sideboards and desks.

EMPIRE BED WITH PINEAPPLE POST

One of the greatest changes which the Empire period produced was in the size and form of beds. From the pleasing, slender dignity of Sheraton and Hepplewhite they become overpowering in thickness and confused with carving. To counterbalance this added weight, the posts become very tall.

A great change in interiors took place as a result of this heavy furniture. Homes of necessity increased in size, with the furniture as a scale rather than the human figure. We can readily see the terrific results when this furniture was used in small rooms, as well as the more serious consequences attendant upon the human beings who occupied these generous rooms with their heroic furnishings. A peculiar lack of sensitiveness to proportion appears in the fact that chairs never increased in size as did the other furniture but seemed if anything to become smaller.

It is impossible to call this entire period bad. Much of the carving, although over-large, was exquisitely wrought, and the characteristic details employed in it, the laurel leaf, horn of plenty, and gadrooning, were in themselves beautifully proportioned. And yet, the entire finished effect was that of a conglomerate mass of poorly arranged details, each calling for first attention.

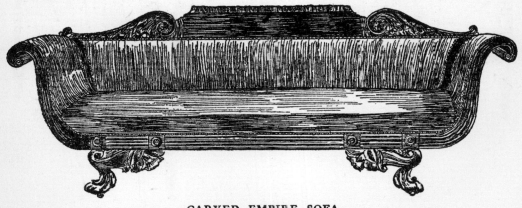

CARVED EMPIRE SOFA

To carry the development of furniture into the carved rosewood era would be to bring this record down to a time within the actual memories of many of us, so we will stop at the Late Empire and leave the Victorian period to speak for itself.

I do not mean that all the furniture that was created about the time of the Civil War was bad, for there were many high lights, yet the shadow caused by failing skill and taste deepened until many of the pieces of furniture became monstrosities of design and color.

We often speak of the horsehair furniture with disdain, because somewhere back in our minds we have the mental picture of the poorly designed and over-carved structures, but let us not forget that many of the fine pieces that were produced in this country before the Revolution had this material for covering.

PHYFE'S WORKSHOP

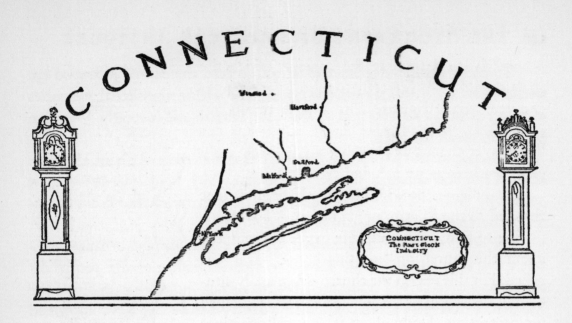

CHAPTER VII

CLOCKS AND CLOCKMAKERS

CLOCKMAKERS of expert craftsmanship are mentioned in the early records of all the colonies, but it remained for those of Connecticut to inspire and establish the trade and make it one of America's first successful industries. The Pilgrims brought no timepieces with them but depended for the approximate hour on nature—the position of the sun and incoming and outgoing tides—and on such crude hourglasses and sundials as they could make. Small sundials of finest workmanship were made in Holland as early as 1600 and we may feel sure that at least one or two such dials were brought over on the *Mayflower*. In construction they consisted of a simple round metal plate with the numerals of the hours engraved on the surface near the circumference and an upright shaft which projected a shadow across the numerals, designating the hour. A compass was added to the pocket type and the whole thing enclosed in a small box for convenient carrying. With the compass it was possible in any place or position accurately to determine the angle at which the shaft should point correctly to record the time. As the years passed these dials were naturally replaced with more accurate clocks, so we shall not linger over them but pass directly to such early clock workers as we can find recorded.

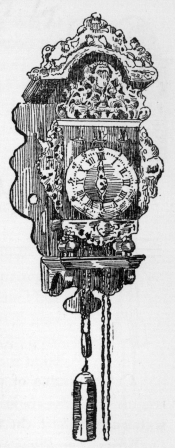

As religious persecution was the greatest fact that led to the Pilgrim immigration, it is not surprising to find community life over here centered about the church or "meeting house," as it was called. For this reason the church was usually situated in the center of the town, and homes grouped for protection closely about it. Here all meetings were held and here in many instances the little bands withstood the attack of hostile Indians, while their homes burned about them. And from here came the first demands for clocks: town clocks for the church belfries. As early as 1704, we read in the records of an Ipswich, Massachusetts, church, that provision was made for the placing of a tower clock, and that in 1740 certain New Haven parishioners refused to pay their quota for the erection of such a clock, as they were distant from

EARLY WALL CLOCK

the church and would be unable to make use of the timepiece. In 1752, a lottery was organized in Philadelphia to raise funds necessary for the completing of the steeple of Christ Church and the purchasing of bells and a clock.

The first recorded name of a clockmaker in this country is that of William Davis, who came here in 1698, no doubt for adventure as well as clockmaking. His family was large, it was impossible for him to support them, and it soon became necessary for David Edwards, a friend of Davis, to give security to the town of Boston that they might not become public charges.

That same year in New Amsterdam, Everardus Bogardus opened a shop and began watch and clockmaking. In 1707, James Batterson advertised in Boston that he had but lately arrived from London and had for sale watches and clocks of his own make. Through nearly all the seaport towns we find clockmakers from London and other European cities establishing their trade at an early date with high hopes of winning their fortunes in the new land.

WAG-ON-THE-
WALL

William Bagnell of Boston at this early period had begun manufacturing eight-day clocks in "hardwood cases," and found a ready market for them. So we may go through long lists of clockmakers whose actual work remains a mystery, but who deserve some mention for attempting to build their trade in the new country and for the ability that they must have had to keep their business through the years in which we know they worked.

In considering the early makers whose authentic works we are permitted to study, the name of William Claggett seems to stand out from those of his contemporaries. His cases were truly inspired by the English makes and his dials were masterpieces of the engraver's art. The author has in his collection an early clock of this maker, that has been in his family since the first part of the Eighteenth Century and is still in running order. Claggett was followed in business by his brother Thomas, who was an equally fine workman and whose clocks are also sought after keenly by collectors.

David Rittenhouse appears at about the same time in Philadelphia, manufacturing not only clocks, but mathematical instruments as well. In private life he was well known as an astronomer and served for a period

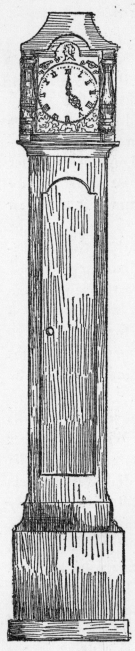

EARLY PINE CLOCK

of years as treasurer of the Pennsylvania colony, as well as director of the mint at Philadelphia in 1779.

Odran Dupuy, another Philadelphia clockmaker, began his trade as early as 1735 and his son John, following in his profession, kept the business running until 1770. In 1734, eight-day clocks with japanned cases were advertised in New York papers by John Bell. Other New York makers of note were John Ent and George Chester, both of whom were working at the same time as Bell.

Thomas Perry, whose shop was in Hanover Square, New York City, with many others of the trade, dealt not only in clocks of his own make but imported others from various European countries to suit the tastes of his clientele. All of these names would mean but little without the early records which prove them to have been craftsmen of great proficiency, for actual clocks from their hands are so scarce as to make their study almost impossible. In the case of the Connecticut workers tradition becomes an actuality.

Thomas Harland, like many of his early contemporaries, came from London and established himself in Norwich, Connecticut. He advertised that he made "in the neatest manner and on the most approved principles, horizontal, repeat and plain watches, in gold, silver, metal or covered cases, spring and plain clocks, church clocks and regulators." He emphasizes strongly that he uses the utmost care in cleaning and repairing watches in the same expert ways then used in London. His price, he points out with pride, is as reasonable as can be obtained abroad.

It was not long before Thomas Harland's fame spread and many ambitious apprentices from all parts of the country applied to him. Among these were men who later became greater then their teacher: Seril Dodge, Henry and Rufus Farnum, William Cleveland, and Eli Terry.

Harland's clocks boasted brass works with forty-inch pendulums moving in a complete arc each second. The brass wheels were made with exquisite care and the works, although simple in construction, were considered as good as those that were imported. Cases for the works were six feet high. So simple in all were these clocks that Harland's apprentices when they left his shop carried with them his methods of manufacturing and in nearly every instance later reproduced his works.

Eli Terry, born in 1772, served a youthful apprenticeship in the shop of Harland and in 1792 made his first signed clock, a grandfather type of simple lines which still is accurately recording the time. We must give credit at this point to Daniel Burnap who taught Terry the art of engraving. Burnap was also a clockmaker, most of his cases being of the grandfather type and containing brass works. A great many of his clocks boasted the calendar and moon attachments; the dials of silver are characteristic in that he never used spandrels.

In 1793 Terry went to Northbury and opened shop. In the same year he married Eunice Warner.

CLOCK BY
WILLIAM CLAGGETT

CLAGGETT
GRANDFATHER CLOCK
146

Terry's early clocks were all made by hand, but it was not long before he employed water power to lighten his work. His prices were high (eight-day clocks selling from thirty-three to forty dollars) so his market was somewhat limited.

Up until this time cases for tall clocks were considered a separate part of the clock and were made by local cabinetworkers to fit specific works. Terry, at the beginning of his career, would make the works of several clocks, strap them to his horse, and in person peddle them throughout the near-by towns.

It was a hand-to-mouth business and we cannot be surprised to find him in 1803 promoting quantity production, assembling machinery, and harnessing more water power. It was a mammoth scheme for the times and he was considered foolhardy for embarking upon his adventure, for news had spread that he had contracted to make as many as four thousand shelf clocks in the succeeding three years. These clocks, it was said, were to have wooden works, running thirty hours without rewinding, second pendulum, dial and hands, all for four dollars. It was, in so many words, the great price-cutting event of that decade. The catch in Terry's agreement was that the purchaser had to supply the materials necessary for the making of the clock.

Some ingenious kink in Terry's mind led him in 1797 to take out a patent on his clock movements, yet this so-seeming protective measure never hindered his rivals when they wished to use his designs.

In 1809, Eli Terry, Seth Thomas, and Silas Hoadley formed a company to manufacture wooden clocks. This company lasted but a year, at the end of which Terry sold out his interest to the other two and went to Plymouth Hollow. Shortly after he withdrew from the firm it was moved to Graystone. Terry continued alone until 1814 when he perfected and patented his second clock. This clock ran thirty hours without rewinding and in construction was distinctive, for he placed the dial works between the plates of the frame instead of between the front plate and the dial.

Another novelty appearing in this clock was the mounting of the verge on a steel pin inserted in one end of a short arm with a screw passing through the other end into the front plate. We find in all the early clocks made of wood that the pin was inserted in a bottom, midway between the center and the periphery. By turning this bottom the verge was adjusted to the escapement wheel.

One of Terry's cases for the new patent was a pillar-and-scroll-top type. It stood some twenty-five inches high and the top and feet were scrolled. At either side was a round pillar three quarters of an inch in thickness that extended the entire height of the case. The dial was eleven inches across, with painted spandrels filling the corners. A painted glass panel in the lower part of the door, below the dial, added distinction to the case. Terry's methods of making these clocks seem most primitive. At first the wheels and teeth were cut with a saw and jackknife after the parts had been marked out with squares and compass. Great accuracy and patience were needed to finish a clock with the speed and precision that marked Terry's work.

His two sons, Eli, Jr., and Henry, came to the factory at Plymouth in 1814 to learn their father's business, and worked with him there for a period of years. The patents which Eli, Sr., had taken out were widely copied by his followers but Terry's work was not limited to small shelf clocks, for it is recorded that he made several steeple clocks and other large instruments for public buildings. He remains the first outstanding clockmaker of Connecticut, and the keen business sense which led him to realize the possibilities that lay in increased production established him as the dean of his profession.

Seth Thomas was given a position in Terry's short-lived company, "Terry, Thomas, and Hoadley," for his ability in making cases. His education had been short and at an early age he was forced by circumstances to earn his living. After serving an apprenticeship as a carpenter and joiner in New Haven, he returned to Northburyport and began work as a joiner

BRACKET CLOCK BY ELI TERRY

in Terry's factory, making cases and assembling works. His rise was rapid and he soon became a foreman in the shop and later, with Hoadley, was taken into the firm. It probably fitted in with Terry's advanced ideas on production that Thomas should do the joinery work and fit together the cases which he himself should cut out.

While in business with Hoadley alone, Thomas made almost entirely long-case clocks. In 1813, he sold his interest to his partner and went to Plymouth to carry on the work for himself. Perhaps it was Terry's new invention that led him in 1814 to drop the manufacture of long-case clocks and turn his ability into the new, popular shelf clock.

The business grew, and in the place of the twenty men whom he employed at the shop there were soon nine hundred. To-day the Seth Thomas factory is still manufacturing some of our best-known clocks. Thomas died in 1859 and his business was incorporated by his two sons, Aaron and Seth, Jr.

Silas Hoadley, third member of the triumvirate of great clockmakers, carried on his business after Terry and Thomas withdrew until 1849, when he rented his shop and closed his business. Hoadley was born in Bethany, Connecticut, in 1786, and like many of the younger generation of the time began his apprenticeship at an early age. He learned the carpentry trade from his uncle and because of his proficiency was given a place in the Terry and Thomas firm. He was not as gifted in inventive ability as were his partners but he worked diligently, gaining a reputation and retiring with sufficient money to support himself comfortably.

The names of Luther and Samuel Hoadley with Riley Whiting should be noted as one of the early firms still doing business. In 1807, they began manufacturing wooden works not unlike those of Terry and Thomas. Luther Hoadley died and Samuel retired, leaving the business in the hands of Whiting. Whiting enlarged it considerably and in 1841 sold to Clarke and Gilbert Company, who still continue the manufacture of clocks under the name of "Gilbert Manufacturing Company." It was Whiting's ability to foresee the demand for eight-day clocks that caused him to enlarge his shop that he might increase his production in this line. Throughout New England to-day we find numbers of the clocks which he made at this time.

The next great step in clock manufacture was introduced by Chauncey Jerome. He, like Hoadley, began as an apprentice and after many years

PILLAR
BRACKET CLOCK

of hard struggle, winning and losing fortunes in his profession through poor business associations, died poor.

In 1812, he went to New Jersey with Lewis Stebbins to whom he had been apprenticed and made tall case clocks for him. Here he remained for one winter and then enlisted for service in the War of 1812. Upon his discharge, at the age of twenty-one, he began work with Eli Terry. He took on many of Terry's ideas of successful clock manufacture and in 1821 sold his home in Plymouth to Terry and took his payment in clocks, rather than in cash. He moved to Bristol where he bought another house with the clocks which he had received. In this house he set up his shop and a most modern note, a circular saw, was included in his machinery. This circular saw may be said to have led to quantity production as Terry had conceived it.

Jerome formed a partnership with Elijah Darrow and Nobles Jerome and attempted to compete with Terry, but it was not until 1837 that he realized his ambition. In that year he revolutionized the clockmaking industry and placed himself as the foremost clock manufacturer of the day.

He realized that the time had come when foreign trade would consume a great many clocks if he could find some way of making them so that they would not be perishable in the damp sea air while en route. In other words, the moisture which got into them while they were on the sea swelled the wooden works and rendered them ever after irregular as time-keepers. This, together with his inability to produce in quantity, caused Jerome much worry. In time his inventive mind devised a machine that could cut wheels from rolled brass in great numbers at one operation. The wheels and plate holes were stamped out by machinery and the manual effort back of clockmaking thereby greatly reduced. With the reduction of labor involved, price automatically fell, and it is recorded that these clocks sold for the small sum of two dollars. The pinions used were all of one kind and known as "lantern pinions," while their leaves were made of pieces of wire set around an axis in two collars. It must be understood that while Terry made brass clocks they were cut or filed by hand from solid blocks of brass and the process was tedious and painstaking. In 1850, Jerome formed a stock company in New Haven, known as the Jerome Manufacturing Company, which lasted but five years and then failed disastrously. It is interesting to remember that P. T. Barnum of circus fame was associated with the company and was forced to pay some of its debts. Jerome's career was brilliant, yet he died a financial failure.

Another name closely associated with the clock industry at this time was Hiram Camp. Camp was born in Plymouth in 1811, at the time when Terry formed his first partnership. Blessed with more than the average amount of inventive ability, he had as well a keen business sense and we find him early in middle life president of one of the largest clock companies in New Haven.

Elias Ingraham, stylist, was inspired by a trip abroad to design the sharp Gothic clock which is so familiar to us under the name of "steeple clock." The pattern of it was simple, having a symmetrical peak rising between two pillars which terminate in graceful pinnacles. Other clocks by

TYPICAL EXAMPLES OF   BY CONNECTICUT AND
EARLY CLOCKS   MASSACHUSETTS
                         MAKERS

BRACKET CLOCK SHOWING LATE EMPIRE
INFLUENCE

this same designer are known under his own names for them: "Doric,"
"Grecian," and "Ionic."

Before we leave the Connecticut manufacturers we must mention the

PILLAR CLOCK SHOWING EMPIRE
INFLUENCE

names of Hiram and Heman Weldon of Plymouth, G. and E. Bartolomew of Bristol, Alcott Cheney of Middletown, Benjamin Cheney of Manchester, Benjamin Hanks of Litchfield, and Enos Doolittle of Hartford. Each contributed noteworthy clocks, but none as distinctive and inspired as those of Terry, Thomas, or Jerome. Their works seem to fall at a late date; nevertheless to them is due all credit for having made the clock a commodity at a price within the reach of all, and from a trade of itinerant peddlers establishing a successful manufacturing industry.

Even at an early date there was great rivalry between Connecticut and Massachusetts in the manufacturing of clocks. Terry and Thomas both caused a slump in the Boston industries when they undersold all their competitors. But we must remember that Simon Williard was making clocks in Boston before Terry was born. Simon was without doubt the best known of his family although his brother, Benjamin Williard, Jr., was the first to take up clockmaking as a trade. The latter made, as we may gather from his own works, "clocks of every sort" in the newest form and warranted to measure time without variation and to go many years without cleaning. Also "clock cases made at the same place in various forms, and in the best manner, and cheaper than can be purchased in London, and conveyed with clocks to any part of the country." The *Massachusetts Spy* in 1774 gives an account of a special sale of Benjamin Williard musical clocks, which, Williard boasts, "will play a different tune every day in the week, and on Sunday a Psalm tune."

Simon Williard, the most illustrious of the brothers, was without a doubt the best clockmaker. He went to school at Grafton and began his apprenticeship with an English clockmaker named Morris. He was assisted by his brother and when thirteen made a tall clock with all the works filed by hand. His mechanical genius was recognized by his brother, and as soon as he finished his apprenticeship he was taken into his brother's shop. Here he remained but a short time, and then went in for himself. On the twenty-seventh of November, 1779, he married Hannah Williard, his cousin. She died a year later and Simon moved to Roxbury. He set up a shop which is now 2196 Washington Street, and a short time later remarried. His work is aptly summed up in his own label, which he placed in his clocks:

Simon Williard, at his clock Dial in Roxbury Street, manufactures every kind of clock work, such as large Clocks for Steeples, made in the best manner, and warranted, price with one dial, 500 dollars; with two dials, 600 dollars, with three dials,

700 dollars; with four dials, 900 dollars. Common eight-day clocks with very elegant faces and mahogany cases, price 50 to 60 dollars. Elegant eight-day timepieces, price 30 dollars. Timepieces which run thirty hours and warranted, price 10 dollars. Spring clocks of all kinds, price 50 to 60 dollars. Clocks that will run one year, with once winding up, with very elegant cases, price 100 dollars. Timepieces for Astronomical purposes, price 70 dollars. Timepieces for meeting houses, to place before the gallery, with neat enamelled dials, price 55 dollars. Chime clocks that will play six tunes, price 120 dollars. Perambulators are also made at said place, which can be affixed to any kind of wheel carriage, and will tell the miles and rods exact, price 15 dollars.

Gentlemen who wish to purchase any kind of clocks are invited to call at said Williard's Clock Manufactory, where they will receive satisfactory evidence, that it is much cheaper to purchase new, than old and second-hand clocks; he warrants all his work—and as he is ambitious to give satisfaction—he doubts not of receiving the public approbation and patronage.

Simon Williard began his business in a small way, making his clocks in winter and peddling them along the North Shore in summer. He did not make cases or dials, as many suppose. The dials were usually of iron, but sometimes of wood, and painted with eight or ten coats to give them an enamel-like appearance. We find that most of his cases were made by such men as Henry Williard of Roxbury and Charles Crehore of Dorchester. The faces were in most instances the work of Charles Bullard.

In 1801, Williard invented the eight-day banjo clock and a year later patented the style. From then on we find him practically discontinuing the manufacture of long-case clocks. In this same year his fame so spread that he was given the commission to make a clock for the United States Senate in Washington. The principles of the mechanism which he made were so new that he had to go to Washington in person to set the clock in position and show how it was to be run. Seven hundred and seventy dollars and his expenses were paid Williard for the clock, a seemingly high price for the times. Sad to say, in 1814, this instrument was destroyed by the British when they burned the city, and we are forced to draw upon our imaginations concerning it. When Williard was hanging this clock in Washington he made the acquaintance of Thomas Jefferson and the latter was so impressed by his ability that he later gave him a commission for a turret clock for the University of Virginia at Charlottsville. In 1837, we find him

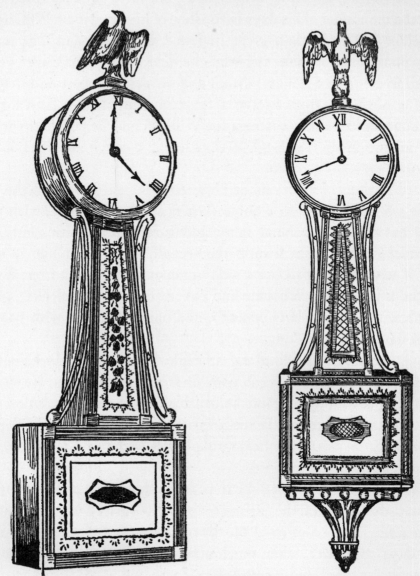

MASSACHUSETTS BANJO CLOCKS

again in Washington, installing other clocks, but in 1839 he returned home and spent the remainder of his days in the shop of his son, Simon Williard, Jr.

The elder Williard was a great inventor and craftsman, but an uncommonly poor business man, and when he died, we find his estate valued at less than five hundred dollars. Proud and sensitive, honest and diligent, he worked at his bench from twelve to fourteen hours a day. Paul Revere, the great silversmith, made castings for Williard and helped him with his improved invention of the English clock-jack, a mechanical device for roasting meat over an open fire

Williard's tall clocks were made between 1780 and 1802, and the later banjo type we may divide into three classifications. The first, with plain mahogany cases and occasional inlay and carved brass ornaments, but without brackets and glass fronts; the second, which he made in great numbers, of mahogany with brass side ornaments and glass front but no bracket; the third (more elaborate and called presentation clocks), gilded and carved, with fine brackets beneath, and painted glasses with pastoral scenes and floral and fret designs.

Seldom, if ever, did Williard use an eagle to top off his clocks, and he never depicted the naval battles so popular with other makers. He showed little sympathy toward the American cause either in the Revolution or in the War of 1812, although it is recorded that he marched with Captain Aaron Kimball from Boston to Lexington, but served only a week and then returned to his business.

Williard made during his life, it is said, about five thousand time-pieces. His early clocks of the eight-day striking variety were cut out by hand with a file from hammered blocks of brass. Tall clocks he made in about six days, and later, when machinery was obtained, turned out one a day without the case. He invented the alarm clock in 1819, and also machinery for turning lighthouse turrets. He was a mechanical genius, and many of his inventions have yet to be improved upon. In August, 1848, he died, in his ninety-sixth year.

Williard's younger brother Aaron began selling his clocks on the South Shore and in a short time through his remarkable business ability had a well-established trade. He built a factory on Washington Street in Boston and with it a group of homes for his workmen, making the neighborhood distinctly a clock district. Thirty men were in his employ, each of whom was a specialist in his line. He copied many of his brother's patterns and his tall case clocks almost without exception are duplicates of Simon's.

Although his clocks were slightly inferior to those of his talented brother they made up for the deficiency in decorative effects. Aaron's son, Aaron, Jr., continued his father's business and invented the lyre-type banjo, which earned him fame and success.

Simon Williard's second son, Simon, Jr., was born in 1795. At the age of fourteen he left school and went to work at a bench in his father's factory. It was not long before he became restless there and entered West Point. In 1816, upon finishing his four years there, he went to New York to study watchmaking, and did not return to Boston until 1828. In the *Columbian Sentinel* in that year he advertises, "New Watchmaking establishment, Simon Williard, Jr., has taken the office lately occupied by Zebedee Cook, Jr., Esq., Rogers Buildings, No. 9 Congress Street, and will be happy to attend the watchmaking business in all its branches. Having been absent some time for the express purpose of availing himself of the information of those most skilled in the profession, he feels a confidence that he shall be able to give satisfaction to all who may honor him with their patronage. Chronometers, Duplex Virgule, Lepine, Horizontal, Repeating, and Patent-lever Watches repaired. Also chimney and musical clocks. Clocks of all descriptions can be obtained from his Father's (Mr. Simon Williard) Factory at short notice."

Benjamin Williard, Simon's fifth son, also went into the clockmaking business and showed considerable skill in mechanical methods. Among Williard's apprentices appear the names of many men who later became as famous in the profession as their talented teacher. Elnathan Taber of

Roxbury (1784–1854) was one of the best of these and when the elder Williard retired, bought his tools and the goodwill of his business.

Lemuel Curtis, born in Boston in 1790, improved the Williard movement for banjo clocks and in 1816 took out a patent on the new works. He moved to Burlington, Vermont, in 1818 and made splendid examples of presentation clocks, very much gilded and ornamented for their time. He used as a rule a round instead of a square case for the pendulum and made the bottom glass convex, with classical paintings.

Let us at this point call attention to the clocks of Philander and Alexander Williard of Ashby, for they are often confused with those of the other Williard family, and were in no way so fine in workmanship as the clocks of their namesakes.

Another capable craftsman whom we should note was Samuel Mulliken, of Newburyport. Born in 1720, at the age of thirty he set up shop and repaired and made clocks until his death six years later. His son Jonathan carried on the business until his death, when a nephew, Samuel, Jr., took it over. Chime clocks playing as many as seven tunes upon twelve bells, watches, and tall clocks were the chief output of this shop, and with great pride the son scorned English competition and rated his eight-day and common one-day clocks far superior to those that were imported. His tall-case clocks were usually of mahogany and had dials of engraved glass. The silhouette of the case itself was not unlike those of Williard's.

Daniel Balch was another clockmaker of Newburyport, and his shop was known as "Sign of the Clock, Newburyport." Here he made chime clocks of four tunes and eight-day clocks and watches. It is more than probable that he did a flourishing business in that seaport town, for the sea captains were usually wealthy and easy spenders. Engraved brass faces with carved spandrels graced Balch's clocks, and the careful designing of the hands is a feature worthy of consideration. His sons, Daniel, 2nd, and Thomas kept up the same quality of work when they succeeded to the business.

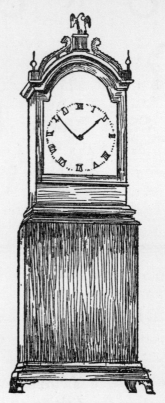

MANTEL CLOCK

David Wood opened a shop in the same town in 1792, and is to be remembered for his so-called "Massachusetts" pattern, which looks like a long-case clock reduced in dimensions. Its height is but approximately thirty-two inches, and the other dimensions were decreased in proportion.

Other contemporary clockmakers include Daniel and Nathaniel Munroe, and Benjamin Bagnall, Jr.

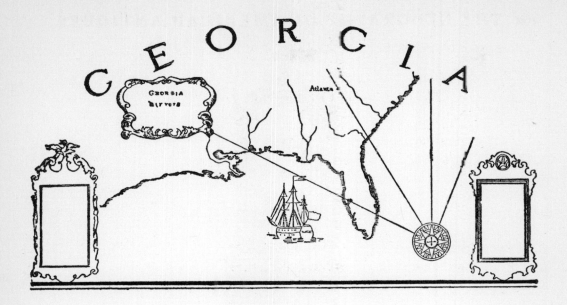

CHAPTER VIII

MIRRORS

THE very earliest mirrors were far from flattering in their reflections, for they consisted of a simple well-polished piece of metal, and in this form they existed for countless generations. It is odd to note that not until the middle of the Seventeenth Century was the looking-glass given a place of any importance whatever in the home, and even a century later they were selling in the American colonies for anywhere from forty to a hundred and fifty pounds. This price was prohibitive enough to keep them out of all homes but those of the wealthy.

One of the earliest mirror enterprises in England was established in London during the reign of George II and known as Vauxhall. This business was owned by the Duke of Buckingham, who imported Venetian glass-makers to supervise it. The reflecting quality of the Vauxhall glasses was obtained by a sheet of tinfoil thinly coated with mercury and stuck to the glass by pressure. All of these mirrors were beveled but the glass, about half the thickness of that which we use to-day, did not permit a deep beveling.

Nearly all of the mirrors that we find in the American colonies prior to 1750 contained imported glass and most of it was Vauxhall. Other mirrors were imported from Italy, or brought in as gifts by travelers and sailors, although we find several unsuccessful attempts to make mirrors locally, notably in Virginia, Massachusetts, and New Jersey. The Italian mirrors are easily distinguished, as their frames were ornate, made of olive wood in an ovolo molding that was often gilded or painted. The English mirrors were square in shape and veneered in small cross-sections in olive wood or walnut upon a walnut base. The molding is characteristic, with a narrow ovolo at the outer and inner edges and a broad molding between. The top extended above the frame in a half circle and was ornamented with exquisite marquetry or with seaweed fret cutting.

Due to the fact that it was impossible at the time to make a piece of mirror larger than forty-five inches in its greatest dimension, we find the earliest glasses small in size. For many years they remain square in shape.

Just when and where the first mirror glass was made in this country is problematical. I have in my collection a rather lengthy though simple set of directions for making glass in the home, which leads me to believe that a great part of the glass that we find in the locally made mirrors of the Seventeenth Century was made, as was everything else, in the home, by home methods. Vauxhall mirror was costly and adorned only the wealthiest homes, yet we find that in New England at an early date there were mirrors consisting of a simple pine board upon which a piece of mirror is held by a small molding. We also find records of glass factories making glass to be used for mirrors, but never a record of anyone who did the silvering, prior to 1739, when George Robinson of Massachusetts and a Mr. Burbeck of Boston were both employed in this occupation. I believe, when we consider the crudeness of some of the earliest looking-glass, that we are justified in calling it home-made, and certainly the frame of this early New

EARLY PINE MIRROR

England mirror bespeaks home workmanship. Reduced to the most simple form, it consisted of a small flat piece of wood, usually pine, upon which the mirror was held by small strips of wood or molding overlapping the glass and pegged to the back board. At top, bottom, and sides the back board protruded beyond the molding and was sometimes shaped, though often plain. A single large inch-thick board pegged across the glass in back held it into the frame. This crude mirror filled the need for the New Englander at the time when the wealthier settlers of Virginia were importing the Vauxhall glasses that we mentioned before.

It is interesting to note in this connection that we find more records around 1650 of mirrors in greater quantity in this country than in England. Inventories mention hazily "walnut-tree glass," "two looking glasses," and so on.

Around 1700 the style changes to a tall, narrow glass with a slightly molded, cross-banded frame. The top is shaped with cyma and ogee curves, mitered at the joinings, as was the frame proper. In some examples of this type a cresting is carried beyond the upper edge of the frame and

TYPICAL
JIG-SAW MIRRORS

jig sawed. Metal brackets for candles were often affixed to the frame and occasionally we find the entire frame gilded.

The jig-saw mirror persisted in America in various forms and sizes for more than a century. The cruder farmhouse pieces were simply constructed, the frame being one piece of wood, jig-sawed at the top and bottom or at only the top and bound next to the glass by a narrow molding. The opening was grooved at the back to permit the glass to sink partially into the frame while the molding about the front of the opening prevented it from falling out. The back was then sealed with a single strip of board

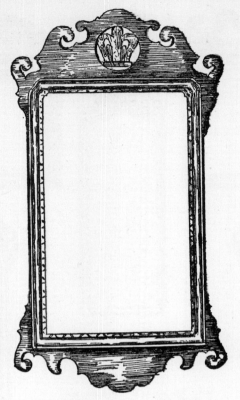

CHIPPENDALE MIRROR

extending over the opening on each side. The more pretentious mirrors of this type were constructed in a similar fashion but we find the corners of the molding rounded and the inmost side of the frame where it meets the glass embellished with narrow gilded bands. The center of the cresting was often broken with a cut-out circle into which was set a gilded gesso eagle or three-plume motif.

Between 1725 and 1745 was introduced a long, low, tripartite glass to rest on mantels, the frame of which was wood gilded, or ornamented with architectural details, scrolled or plain. The joinings of the three pieces of glass were covered with a molding. These mirrors are more properly classed with wall mirrors than with the hanging variety, and seem to have been

MIRROR OF THE LATTER
HALF OF THE SEVEN-
TEENTH CENTURY

COURTING MIRROR

more common in the great manor houses of Maryland and Virginia than in New England.

During this period the first dressing-glasses
were produced. Such glasses were attached by a
screw to turned or plain uprights, which ran into a
small box fitted with several small drawers. Many
of these mirrors were veneered, others inlaid, and
we can find a few examples where the actual frame
of the glass was jig sawed or shaped, similar to the
contemporary hanging mirrors. The dressing-glass,
we gather from letters and wills, was a popular and
well-received gift.

About 1745 American craftsmen made a
rococo gilt mirror that so closely simulated the
Italian mirrors of the time that only by minutely
detailed examination can we discern the differences.
In outline they were irregular though still retaining
rectangular shapes. A wooden frame made the
foundation upon which a restless arrangement of
scrolls and foliage was built up in gesso—i.e., a
composition plaster worked on a wooden or bent-
wire foundation. The irregular shape of these mirrors on the inner as well as the outer side prevented
beveling.

The next stage of development gave us probably as fine a mirror as any that our craftsmen
have produced. It has a broken pediment upon an
architecturally detailed architrave. Below the top
is a molding with projected square corners that
carry down the sides and into a scrolled bottom
apron. The inner edges of the molding are delicately

carved and gilded, as is also the narrow molding directly adjacent to the glass. The architrave is carved with the egg-and-dart or other architectural motifs, and gilded. The scroll of the broken arch is gilded and ends in a small rosette with pendent leaves, at times also gilded. A gesso fillet is suspended from the corner of the square molding at either side. Below the pediment may or may not be carved and gilded ornaments. In the center of the broken arch we find a gilded urn, a shell, an eagle, or the Prince of Wales's plumes. The wealth of delicate carving and the cautious use of gilt against a beautiful piece of cherry, walnut, or mahogany veneer give a beauty to these mirrors that is unrivaled by any others.

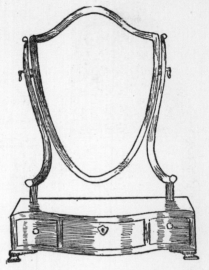

SERPENTINE-FRONT DRESS-
ING-GLASS

During the middle years of the Eighteenth Century, as Wren architecture was introducing a new spirit into the interiors of America as well as those of England, we find mirrors becoming an integral part of wall paneling or made in the hanging variety, with refined architectural detail and carving. Actual designs from the hands of Sir Christopher Wren and Robert Adam are known to have existed and for many years to have been widely copied in the colonies and elsewhere.

SWELL-FRONT DRESSING-GLASS

A GILT MIRROR

An interesting and lovely mirror that seems to have been comparatively common during the latter years of the Eighteenth Century is known as the filigree looking glass. The ornamentation of such mirrors was made of gesso upon a wire foundation. Rectangular in shape, the molding of the frame, often carved, ran clear around the glass. At the crest stood an urn from which extended scrolls of leafy branches and flowers. The urn was often fluted and there were medallions and rosettes in the floral scrolls.

ORNATE CHIPPENDALE MIRROR

In the American mirrors fashioned after Chippendale as well as those of the master craftsman himself, we find a lack of restraint that often gives a quality of ostentation. Usually of gilt and rococo in their treatment, they stand in sharp contrast to the more severe architectural styles which preceded them. "C" curves in prominence, vases, medallions, scrolls, ribbons, shells, pheasants, temples, and fretwork are used in a gamut of woods and finishes. Between the actual frame of the mirror and the glass are often inserted smaller pieces of mirror, surrounded with or-nate narrow moldings similar to the frame. This added to the feeling of delicacy that predominates throughout this style because of the restless arrangement of detail, the extreme narrowness of all visible portions of the frame, and the refinement of the carving.

A more common type of Chippendale style mirror found in this coun-try is the jig saw, differing from all others of the same class in that the scrolls employed curved toward the outside of the frame and the "C" formed thereby always faces the glass.

Toilet mirrors following the styles of the Chippendale, Sheraton, and Hepplewhite become shaped and the supports carved. In some instances the box is made serpentine, blocked, or *bombé* in shape.

The tripartite overmantel mirror was popular with this school of designers. Acanthus scrolls, fretwork, tropical birds, and Chinese temples, all in delicately wrought gesso, make these mirrors genuinely ornate.

Another mirror found in many New England seaport towns is com-monly called, and with no apparent logical reason, the "courting mirror." Problematical as these are, they seem to be of Chinese origin and may have first been brought here by sea captains; but at best they remain an interest-ing exotic note in early furnishings. Owing to the abundant use of small glass, we find them almost without exception fastened with removable pegs into a small flat box and in this box they remained when hung on the wall. Nearly square in proportion and varying in size from eight by ten inches to twelve by fourteen, they were made of a square of mirror com-pletely framed with half-inch strips of painted glass of various lengths. These small pieces were glued to the backing and hemmed on either side and at their joinings with narrow strips of molding. At the top a geometric shape of three or five sides formed a cresting for the mirror. The containing box did not follow this shape at the top, but remained rectangular. Floral or geometric designs of varying degrees of crudeness and perfection were painted upon the back of the border glasses.

BALBOA MIRROR WITH
MARBLE FRAME

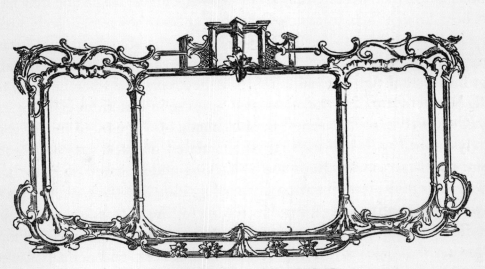

CHIPPENDALE GILT MIRROR

173

CONVEX GIRANDOLE MIRROR

Another form of mirror which seems to be a foreigner in America and, like the courting mirror, found usually in seaport towns, is the Balboa or "bilboa." In this instance the frame is made entirely of colored marble. On the sides are marble columns with gilded finials and feet, and at the top a large medallion or urn supported by gilded scrolls of leaves and flowers. These mirrors supposedly came from Portugal.

The reversion to classical simplicity through the French mode directly following the American Revolution caused a great change in the mirrors of the day. All the flowing line of the jig-saw and Chippendale glasses is

EMPIRE MIRROR WITH PAINTED
DECORATION

EMPIRE TABERNACLE
MIRROR

consigned to complete oblivion and replaced with severe, formal, neo-classicism. Black and gold predominate over wood finishes and add to the formal atmosphere. Two types stand out alone in this period, namely the girandole and the more common "tabernacle" mirror.

The girandole mirror was framed in a deep molding of gilt and black. The fillet of black ran next to the glass and in the hollow deep gilt molding the supposedly symbolic thirteen balls were placed at regular intervals. The top was surmounted by an eagle, flame, or dolphin. In some cases where the eagle was used, strings of prisms were suspended from his beak and carried to candle sconces that were inserted in the side of the frame.

The tabernacle mirror, so called by some authorities and dubbed by others merely Empire mirror, was found in every home about the time of the War of 1812 and in many instances bore paintings depicting great naval and land battles of the war. The frame is rectangular with beveled cornice and pilasters superimposed upon the sides. A third or less of the mirror space at the top is covered with a painting on glass or a solid piece of gilded wood displaying carved fruit, foliage, or other typical Empire motifs. On a few rare examples the eagle and thirteen stars are symbolically painted or carved. In the early and sometimes ungilded tabernacle mirrors small acorns are set into and below the cornice. Later gilded balls replace the acorns. The pilasters at the sides often are mere strips of molding, at other times classical columns, fluted, rope-turned, or plain.

As time goes on these mirrors deteriorate, losing the architectural cornice but retaining a semblance of the columnar treatment. In this stage the simulated column runs around all four sides of the frame and rosettes mark each corner. Sections of the columns were gilded and other parts painted black. At best, these mirrors were heavy in appearance and retained no vestige of the grace that characterized the earlier ones.

Cheval glasses, that is, dressing-table glasses without the box, were made in the early part of the Nineteenth Century but were never in common use. Usually they had a heavy, severe frame, with the two side panels lower than the center one and were hinged so as to be movable and fold away.

Mirror glass was used from an early date to back sconces, but more for reflecting quality than for service as mirrors, so we shall consider them in the chapter on lighting equipment rather than here.

So down through the years we can see in the mirrors reflections of the shapes and forms of contemporary furniture.

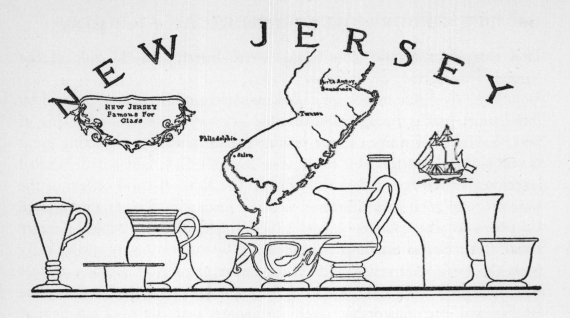

CHAPTER IX

GLASS

It seems hard to realize that the glass which we consider an absolute necessity was one of the great luxuries in the early days of the settlement of this country. For general use dishes were fashioned of wood or pewter and oiled paper or wooden panels were the substitutes for window glass. Fortunate indeed was the possessor of a glass bottle or a bit of windowpane. The need for glass became so acute that the colonists, finding it nearly impossible to obtain it by import, were forced to attempt its manufacture in this country. And so we find the very first manufacturing industry established in the American colonies in the form of a successful glass house started by Caspar Wistar in Salem County, New Jersey, in 1739. The settlement itself and the well-known glass which it produced were called Wistarburg after their founder and originator.

This was by no means the first attempt at glass making in the colonies.

It is recorded that two glass houses were established near Jamestown, Virginia, one in 1607 and another in 1621, used mainly as a mint for the manufacture of glass beads for Indian trade. Both of these factories fell into disuse, partly through the difficulty in keeping skilled workmen and also because the vicinity did not provide the proper kind of sand for glass manufacture. In 1639, glass works were established in Salem on a much larger scale than ever before in America. Crude bottles and small wares were made in great quantities but soon the place closed for lack of funds. Unsuccessful attempts were made in New Amsterdam and Pennsylvania, about this time, to establish the industry. Transportation facilities were poor, the roads were worse, and the wagons which served as conveyances were springless; fuel and good sand were not always found in the same locality and often one or both were far enough removed from one of the settlements to make their use impossible or the obtaining of them a dangerous risk, so it was more than a century before glass making was begun in earnest and put on a business basis.

The people in general had very little money to spend on anything but the barest necessities and the few wealthy preferred to import glass, or crystal as it was often called, from Europe, where the art of glass making had reached a more advanced stage of perfection.

The glass blowers were a roving lot, going from place to place, and it is only natural to suppose they carried the methods and technique of one glass house to another. The glass house had a melting pot, usually in a corner, in which bits of metal for making glass were thrown. Workmen who had artistic ability were encouraged to try their skill in making original designs. They were allowed, after hours, to make for themselves whatever struck their fancy. This may account for some of the odd pieces of glass that are difficult to classify.

The first American products were chiefly bottles and window glass. The bottles were of a coarse texture, generally green in color, and with the surface full of bubbles. The mouth had an irregular edge with no rim;

this was caused by cutting the neck of the bottle with a scissors-like instrument while the glass was still soft.

The pontil mark, which is found on the base of old blown glass, is the round, rough scar left on the object after it had been broken from the pontil rod. This rod enabled the workmen to hold the glass securely while finishing the top. As methods improved the mark was ground down smooth. Shortly after 1850 the pontil mark disappeared completely, the base of the bottle was smooth and hollow, and a rim was added to the mouth. Later we find the base flat and smooth.

The melting pots were made of a particular kind of clay which was ground to a powder and mixed with a certain proportion of burnt clay. Water was added and the mass thoroughly kneaded and then kept damp for some time before starting to build the pot. This building up of the clay in rings or layers, keeping the sides smooth and free from cracks, having the right amount of moisture while working it and then letting it dry out at night was a tedious process. After it was completed it was allowed to stand several months to dry out and finally was put in a kiln and heated until red hot. It was then put in the furnace and was ready for use. The raw materials, silica, an alkali, and one or more other ingredients, were put in and melted or fused, the impurities removed, and then allowed to cool until the molten mass or "metal" was no longer in a liquid state but could be gathered up on a blowpipe. The "gatherings" were then blown either "offhand" or in a mold. "Offhand" blowing required considerable skill and artistic ability to produce a beautiful piece of glass. One-piece molds were used for pieces where the top was the largest part, such as bowls and jars. When a piece was smaller at the top or had a curved outline it was necessary to blow it in a two- or three-piece mold. These molds were hinged, some opened vertically and others hoizontally. Mold-blown glass was very apt to have a seam where the sections joined together unless the mold was new or very tightly fitted. It is the three-mold glass that is in such demand by collectors at the present time. The patterns were cut in intaglio on the inside surface of the molds and as the plastic glass was blown in the air forced it to follow the design. When the piece of glass was removed from the mold every protuberance on its surface had a corresponding depression inside unless the "metal" had not been of the proper temperature or the "gathering" had been too large.

Pressed-glass molds resembled the blown-glass molds, but instead of the metal being blown in against the pattern it was pressed by a plunger into all the crevices of the mold. By this method the finished piece was smooth on the inside no matter how deeply cut the pattern on the outside may have been. The patterns as a rule have a stippled background and are much more intricate and elaborate than those used for the three-mold glass.

Three-mold glass pieces had certain distinctive patterns that made them quite easily recognized. The simplest form of decoration was ribbing that varied in width and length, and was either horizontal, vertical, twisted diagonal, or herringbone. Sometimes it was combined with sunbursts, which were frames, square or rectangular, with lines radiating to the sides from a center. Fluting was popular, and so was diamond diapering in which the diamond-shaped protuberances formed an all-over pattern. Another favorite was the equilateral diamond in a square or rectangular frame. With these five patterns any number of combinations could be made. For the more elaborate patterns the scroll, curve, and arch were used as motifs.

To Caspar Wistar is due much credit for establishing the industry in this country. Born in Germany in the latter part of the Seventeenth Century, he came to Philadelphia in 1717. His keen business sense and excellent judgment made him foresee the future of the glass industry, although at the same time he was engaged in making brass buttons and conducted an importing and exporting business as well. He selected a site in Salem County, New Jersey, that offered plenty of fuel within reasonable distance, good sand for his industry, and near-by waterways that would facilitate

WISTARBERG

disposal of his fragile wares. Four skilled workmen he brought from Holland—John Wentzell, Caspar Haltar, John Halton, and Simon Kreismeier—and put them under contract to teach fine glass making to him and his son Richard and to no one else. For this service they were to receive all expenses, support, and one third net profit.

Although the earlier productions of the Wistarberg factory were undoubtedly Dutch in influence, for the most part broad and squat, the sense of heaviness was relieved by the way the light reflected from the surface. The greens and blues, especially in the paler shades, seem unbelievably delicate and clear. The later glass is characterized by a finer feeling for color and form. Though it still expressed a certain crudity it was invariably distinctive.

Wistar was the first to obtain the two- or three-colored pieces by fusing the glass in concentric, waved, or whirled designs. Such combinations as opaque white and emerald-green; brown and emerald-green; clear and opaque white; clear and brown-blue; green and white-blue; amber and clear, were made. Plain colors were the favorites, clear opaque and turquoise, opalescent, dark brown, amber, and greens. Not much dark blue was made.

One of the characteristic marks of Wistar glass is the thin thread of glass that was wound spirally around the neck of a pitcher or top of a bowl. The wave design of decoration was another characteristic. This was obtained by giving a partly finished piece a second coating of glass which while still soft was drawn over the surface to form the design. A corrugated effect was made by simple perpendicular rubbing. The crimped foot is also a characteristic feature.

Some of the earlier and cruder bowls were made of transparent turquoise-blue and there was also a peculiar and quite distinctive bluish opalescent color that was used in smaller articles. Green-brown seemed to be the favorite color and one finds charming sea-green bowls. The pitchers as a rule were green, with a well-rounded body and a flaring neck. Bowls were of all sizes in shades of green, blue, and brown, and like the pitchers either were plain or had superimposed decorations.

Glass balls large and small, plain and colored, were made for covers to the bowls and pitchers and served their purpose well.

At this factory was turned out the first flint glass made in this country, as well as the first bi- and tri-colored glass. Early bowls and pitchers were made of an ugly brown glass and were rough and squat in shape; bottles were heavy with round shoulders, tapering necks, and deep dents in the bottom. They were of many shapes and no two exactly alike.

Practically all types of glassware were turned out by Caspar Wistar's enterprising industry; window glass, lamp glasses, bottles of all sizes; café, snuff, and mustard bottles; bowls, pitchers, and drinking glasses.

Whorls of color and spiral threads run through many of the Wistarberg pieces although the wide range of color that is so characteristic of his work may also be credited to other south Jersey glass plants. We know that Wistar's compatriots left him before long and set up businesses for themselves, and we can not doubt for a second that some of the glass which we know to-day as Wistar was in reality the product of other factories in the same section. Unfortunately, we are in no way able to prove the

EARLY JERSEY GLASS

STIEGEL SUGAR BOWL

matter when the question comes up, but may feel just pride in a piece that resembles Wistarberg enough to be mistaken for it.

With the death of the elder Wistar in 1752, his son Richard took over his father's business, and being a wealthy man and not dependent upon the income of the factory, turned it over to a manager under whom it continued to succeed until 1780, when it was closed forever.

The gay and debonair Baron Stiegel needs no introduction. William Henry Stiegel was born in Germany in 1729. He came to Philadelphia in 1750 and within two years married the daughter of Jacob Huber, owner of

AN EXAMPLE OF STIEGEL GLASS

large iron furnaces in eastern Pennsylvania. His father-in-law took him into partnership and soon he acquired quite a fortune.

Like Wistar, he could foresee a ready market for glass, so in 1763 he began experiments in glass making at Manheim, Pennsylvania. In less than two years he had furnaces built and skilled workmen imported from England and Germany, and was doing business in earnest. He was gay, luxury-loving, and extravagant, living far beyond his means. This led to bankruptcy in 1774, and he was forced to eke out a precarious living as a teacher until his death in 1785.

His first output of glass consisted mainly of window glass and bottles of various sizes and was sold to merchants in the near-by towns of Lancaster,

York, and Reading. Then followed a much finer ware in which subtlety of color, clarity of ring, and traces of refinement are qualities that distinguish it from other American glass.

The early flint glass was light in weight, thin, uniform in color, and brilliant of surface. The enamels on glass were clearer and more brilliant than those made in Europe at the same period. Stiegel made and advertised glass of all kinds, salt cellars, cream pots, sugar bowls, cruets, ink bottles, bowls, candlesticks, sweetmeat and mustard jars, and numerous other articles. Some were made of clear flint glass and others were of colored glass or of translucent or opaque glass, enameled.

Stiegel's favorite color seems to have been the deep blue that is quite unmistakable, but the amethyst, wine, and shades of green are also very beautiful. Amber was also used but not to such an extent as the other colors. We find such combinations as clear flint with amethyst or blue, opaque white with clear or colored flint.

The salt cellars were made in many shapes and those of blue flint glass are especially attractive. While there is not such a variety in shape or color as we find in those made at Sandwich, the outline is softer, showing the difference between blown and pressed, patterned glass.

Drinking glasses of all kinds and descriptions were produced in quantities. They were paneled, engraved, had colored fused decorations, curved and diamond or quilt-shaped patterns. The stems of the wine glasses, both twisted and straight, were much like those made in England, but the foot was flatter and more solid, and the edge turned down and in. Some of the flip glasses were beautifully engraved with flower designs and have the appearance of being too fragile for the hard usage they generally received.

Poor judgment in business brought this factory's history to a close yet its products are more highly treasured than those of any other glass house in America.

In 1802, Hunnewell and Gore of Boston opened a glass house at Chamsford, Massachusetts, now known as Lowell, for the manufacture of window

STIEGEL

glass. When the American ports were closed during the War of 1812 glass-making received another impetus and the venture was successful until 1827, when the works burned down. Later it was rebuilt and again made glassware, but never was the business as profitable and after changing owners several times it was moved to Pembrook, New Hampshire, and finally closed in 1850.

"Success to the Railroad" bottles, commemorating the opening of the Boston and Lowell railroad, were one of their better-known products. These bottles were a poor grade of glass owing to the inferior sand that was used.

The first glass works built at Stoddard, New Hampshire, in 1842 failed, but the second factory was successful. The glass decanters and bottles made there were amber-green, dark, and coarse in texture. Some of the blown pieces were made in three section molds. The quilted and sun-

EARLY NINETEENTH CENTURY BOTTLES

burst pattern found on decanters and bottles is distinctive. A considerable quantity of window glass was also made for the local homes.

The output of the Keene factories at Keene, New Hampshire, consisted principally of bottles that were crude in shape and of dark, coarse glass. Some were plain and others had patriotic and Masonic emblems. "Keene" is found on some and during the ownership of Perry and Wood an eagle and "P.W." were used as embellishments. These works were opened in 1815 and continued under different owners until 1850, and then were abandoned.

The factory at Glassboro, New Jersey, was opened in 1775 by the Sanger brothers, who had formerly been with Wistar. In 1837, after several changes of ownership, it was bought by Thomas H. Whitney. Three years later he and his brother established the firm of Whitney Brothers. This business is still in existence under the name of the Owens Bottle Company of Toledo, Ohio.

EARLY NINETEENTH CENTURY BOTTLES

Though bottles were not the only product of this plant they seem the chief product. The dark-brown whiskey bottle, "booze bottle," in the shape of a log cabin, ink-stands in the shape of beehives or cider barrels were made during the presidential campaign of Harrison in 1840. The Jenny Lind bottle was another favorite originated in 1850. These bottles had a long slender neck and round body. Other firms made them also, and varied the decorations. The Whitney Jenny Lind bottle. however, had a head of the singer in relief on the side.

The glass works at Kensington, Pennsylvania, later known as the Dyottville Glass Works, was established in 1771 and is still in existence. The principal output consisted of bottles, flasks, and demijohns of every description.

One of the outstanding features of the first successful Pittsburg glass house, erected in 1797, was the use of coal for fuel. In other factories before this and long afterward wood was used as a means of heating the furnaces. Besides window glass we find from an old advertisement of 1800 that they made bottles, pocket flasks, pickling jars, apothecary shop furnishings, and other hollow-ware. By 1807 they had added decanters, tumblers, and blue-ware to their list.

By the time decorated flasks became so popular in the early part of the Nineteenth Century we find several glass houses making these. There were three sizes: half pint, pint, and quart, blown in amber, olive-amber, brown, and aquamarine. The bottles made by Frederick Lorenz were initialed by him and were of two types. Later (1851–1860) Lorenz and Wightman made a series of Union flasks with clasped hands and flying eagles on opposite sides. The initials L and W are on the bottom. After 1860 Fahnestock, Albree and Company continued the business, using the mark "F. A. & Co."

The Sandwich Manufacturing Company, later called the Boston and Sandwich Glass Company, was started in 1825 by Deming Jarves, who had formerly been connected with the New England Glass Company of Boston.

SANDWICH

He chose the site at Sandwich, Massachusetts, mainly on account of the quantities of firewood along Cape Cod and its comparative nearness to Boston, a distance of fifty miles by water. The first railroad in Massachusetts was built there, connecting the factory with the dock, which was about half a mile away. The sand found in the locality was not of the kind used in fine glass making, but that seemed to be a minor consideration, for good sand could be obtained from New Jersey and western Massachusetts.

The first glass manufactured here was clear flint, and used for tableware and windowpanes. Later, pressed, cut, and etched glass were made. It would seem that at some time during the existence of the works, with such enormousness of output and diversity of products, every kind of glass article then in use was made. There is no complete list of the output, as very little advertising was done. The demand for the goods was large enough to absorb the supply.

The tale is current that a carpenter wishing to have some glassware of a particular shape conceived the idea of pouring the hot molten glass into a wooden mold and pressing it into the desired shape. Mr. Jarves, with the help of this workman, made experiments that proved the theory was practical. The first mold was a crude wooden affair resembling somewhat a small cider press. It soon became apparent that wood was not the material for molds and metal took its place. Pressed glass was known in Europe some time before the Sandwich experiments; however, it was confined to salt cellars, bowls, and candlesticks. These were plain, with square feet, and crude in construction. At least the Boston and Sandwich Glass Company has the credit of improving the method if not of originating the idea.

The art of opal-glass making was introduced by Rice Harris, an Englishman who was paid by the company to come to Sandwich and teach the workmen the process of making it. He stayed six months and received five thousand dollars for his labors.

The company continued to do business until 1888, when, owing to labor trouble, its factory was closed and was never reopened.

The earlier pieces, made under the supervision of Mr. Jarves, who left the company in 1858, seem superior in quality and design to those made later. Noticeable among these are the cup plates and candlesticks, so dear to the heart of the collector. When oil lamps became the fashion, about the middle of the last century, the company manufactured them in enormous quantities for both domestic and export trade. The earlier lamps were made of clear glass and simpler in design than those of later date.

The output of the factory being so enormous, it would be impossible to name every kind of thing made, but we know there were pitchers, bowls, vases, glasses of all kinds, door knobs, salt cellars, plates and dishes of all sizes, cologne bottles, cruets, candlesticks, lamps, and toilet articles.

Colored glass was introduced about 1830 and used either separately or in conjunction with clear or opaque white. We find black, blue, opal-canary, ruby, and amber. These colors were unequaled by those of any other house of the time. The scarcity of canary glass seems to bear out the fact that it cost more to make that color than it did some of the others. The gold ruby was used principally for lanterns and railroad lights.

Between the years 1860 and 1880 perfume bottles, lamps, toilet sets, and bathware made of white opaque glass were decorated with gold and mineral paints. The lace or snakeskin pattern is characteristic of Sandwich

SANDWICH CUP PLATES

glass, and in the later pieces it is of much more delicate and sparkling design than in the earlier.

The essentials for the successful manufacturing of glass, besides an abundance of raw ingredients and plenty of fuel, were good melting pots, a furnace, and suitable tools to handle the molten glass.

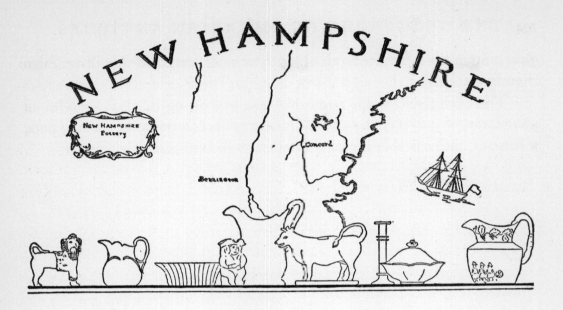

CHAPTER X

POTTERY AND PORCELAIN

FEW records exist that tell anything of the early production of earthenware in this country. Red clay was found in abundance in many sections of the country and we conclude that the early pottery was made of it. The blue clay which was used for stoneware was not so common, hence its use was more restricted.

Clay was dug from the earth in the fall of the year to prepare it for pottery making. It was mixed with water and ground to a fine paste, then allowed to harden in large blocks of about one hundred pounds each, and stored away where it could be kept moist without freezing.

In classifying pottery and porcelains, the earthenware or pottery is opaque and the porcelain or china is translucent. The clay and other substances used in making either group are known as the paste or body. This paste is divided into two groups, the hard and the soft. After the first firing before the glaze is applied the paste is known as biscuit. Literally, the soft paste is no softer than the hard paste to the touch but it will not stand so intense a heat as the latter. Bone china, artificial porcelain, flint enamelware, Rockingham, and all earthenware, yellow or white, slip ware, and sgraffiato are all soft pastes, while fine and coarse stoneware, Parian, stone, and ironstone china are hard pastes. Natural porcelain is made largely of kaolin, a very fine white clay, and feldspar, which is fusible at an intense heat; bone china consists of kaolin, bone, and feldspar; earthenware of clay substances, feldspar, and some quartz; and stoneware of blue clay, feldspar flint. The blue clay, though very strong, will not stand intense heat unless mixed with other substances.

Soft paste utensils were made long before those of hard paste and required less skill in handling than the latter. On account of the porous and absorbent qualities of this paste it was invariably glazed to render it of any practical use whatever. The glaze consisted of a thin mixture (principally of pulverized glass and water) which was put upon the surface of the paste and fused by firing. The lead glaze was produced by applying a liquid containing oxide of lead or by sprinkling the surface with a powder consisting in great part of lead sulphide. Salt glaze was particularly adapted to stoneware, which could be fired at a high temperature. The common way of obtaining this glaze was to put the pottery in the kiln and when the proper heat was reached to throw in the salt. The combination of vapors arising formed a rough coating on the pottery, resembling somewhat the skin of an orange. These glazes were all transparent and permitted the colors of the pastes to be seen through them, so when it was desirable to hide the original color other substances were added to make the glaze opaque. Enamel is a better name to apply to the opaque glazes.

Before 1650 the potters in Virginia were supplying the families living in the immediate vicinity of their primitive kilns with crude earthenware utensils for household use. Bricks, although not classed with pottery and porcelain, formed a great part of the output of these kilns. They were made of the red clay and rendered usable by firing. Throughout Virginia, New

England, and Pennsylvania brick-making industries were established at an early date. By 1647 the business was well developed in Virginia and New England and after 1685 we find record of large brickyards in different sections of Pennsylvania. Great Britain and Holland exported bricks to the colonies but the cost of these was prohibitive. With the clay at hand it was a simple matter to make bricks at a low cost, and the prevalence of great fires led the colonists to employ brick in constructing their homes.

A ware somewhat similar to Holland Delft was made in the early days of the Dutch settlement of New Amsterdam, and in 1735 in the same city John Rammy was making the first stoneware and William and Peter Crolius were making various kinds of pottery. The earliest stoneware made in this country seems to have come from a pottery erected at or near Burlington, New Jersey, in 1684. This enterprise was owned by Daniel Coxe of London, who, after considerable difficulty with his assistants sent from England, sold out his entire interest in 1691. The clay which Coxe used was supposed to have come from South Amboy, New Jersey.

Sgraffiato decorated pottery is almost without exception a unique product of Pennsylvania. The few pieces that it is claimed were made in Jersey and Vermont were never as elaborately decorated as those of Pennsylvania, and appear at a much later date. The methods of making this

EARLY PENNSYLVANIA PLATES OF SGRAFFIATO

EARLY PENNSYLVANIA PLATE WITH FIGURE
DECORATION

crude pottery were brought to Pennsylvania from Germany by the early settlers, and were used here from 1735 to 1850. In general, the sgraffiato pieces were made as gifts and for ornament rather than for practical everyday use. In color the paste was red or dark brown and sometimes yellow, with a slip of lighter color so that when the design was cut or scratched the darker body color would show through. The designs used were as a rule very crude but in effect the finished product was really artistic. The same primitive feeling runs through sgraffiato ware that is found in the carved and painted dower chests of Pennsylvania. David Spinner, a potter of the early Nineteenth Century, produced some unusually lovely slip ware. His designs were more carefully drawn and executed than those of his contemporaries. His great love for floral designs is attested in every dish that he made and the fuchsia seems to have been his favorite motif. John Liedy, who worked at the same time, also produced some exquisite pieces, with the tulip predominant in his designs.

POTTERY EAGLE FROM PHOENIXVILLE,
PENNSYLVANIA

Slip ware is attributed almost entirely to Pennsylvania when in reality almost all potteries at one time or another used slip for decoration. Slip was made by mixing clay with water to the consistency of heavy cream. This mixture was put in a slip cup that ended with one or more hollow tubes through which the slip could run as a design was traced. After a piece of pottery had been fashioned, whether modeled by hand or shaped on a mold, it was set away for a time to permit the water to dry out of the clay. In this state it was said to be "green." When dry enough to be fired without danger of cracking, the slip was applied. The paste quickly absorbed the water in the slip leaving the design of clay raised upon the surface. If the article was intended for decorative use alone the slip was left in this state, but if it were made for practical purposes the design was pressed down to the level of the body. The ware was then warmed and the glaze applied.

On such articles as pie plates, where the top received the hardest usage, the glaze was applied only to that surface and care was taken to have all the edges covered. In crocks and jars both inside and outside were glazed.

This primitive method of slip ware continued generally until the end of the Civil War, when a more satisfactory and serviceable material appeared upon the market, namely, tin, and later, enameled ware. Many examples of the earlier decorated slip ware have on them pictures—or descriptions in words—of historical events, while on the later pie plates given names appear as major units in the designs.

Abraham and Andrew Miller succeeded to the Philadelphia pottery established by their father in 1790. About 1810 the business was removed to another section of the city and Andrew withdrew from the firm. Abraham Miller is supposed to have made the first silver luster ware in this country. He produced as well a great variety of pottery, including Rockingham and decorated tableware. The "Tam O'Shanter" mugs popular toward the middle of the Nineteenth Century he made in Rockingham pottery un-

TUCKER CHINA

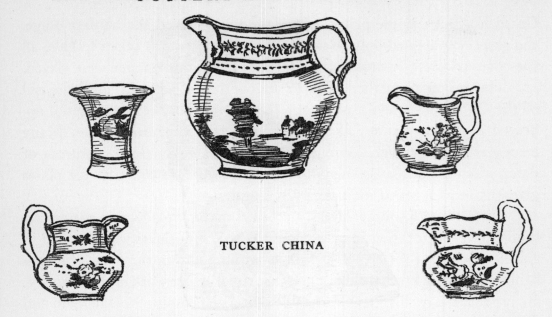

TUCKER CHINA

marked. He conducted several experiments with hard-paste porcelain but never manufactured it for commercial purposes.

William Ellis Tucker, son of Benjamin Tucker, a Quaker, opened a china chop in Philadelphia and experimented in decorating imported white china. This he fired in a small kiln that his father had constructed for him. Later he made simple pottery and feeling that it was not completely satisfactory experimented in producing hard-paste porcelain. After many failures he succeeded in producing a good-quality porcelain. In 1826, he built a factory near Philadelphia and the following year was awarded a medal by the Franklin Institute for the best gold-decorated porcelain made in Pennsylvania. The workmanship of this piece was poor but the paste and glaze were of unusual quality. In 1828, he received a medal for the best porcelain made in the United States and this time the workmanship was of much better type. The name of his firm was now Tucker and Hulme, but in 1829 Hulme withdrew and Tucker continued alone until 1832, when he formed a partnership with Joseph Hemphill. Soon after this Tucker died, and his place in the firm was taken by Robert C. Hemphill. Thomas

BLUE POTTERY DOG FROM
NEW JERSEY

Tucker, son of William Ellis Tucker, was retained as superintendent of the works. Skilled workmen were brought from England and before long the factory was reproducing with considerable accuracy the decorative designs used by the Sèvres factory in France. Much of this ware was left unmarked because of the current feeling throughout this country that the best of everything should be imported and never locally made. Hemphill continued to exhibit his wares and receive favorable commendation until 1832, when Thomas Tucker became proprietor of the business. After a few months of active work he closed the factory.

The ingredients used in the porcelain made in this factory came from far and wide. Kaolin usually was brought from the near-by districts, the blue clay used came from Jersey, and the feldspar from Delaware.

The Jersey Porcelain and Earthenware Company began operations in 1825 at Jersey City, producing both the common yellow and white wares, and besides these they made gold-decorated porcelain of excellent quality.

CONNECTICUT STONEWARE WITH DECORATED AND SCRATCHED
EMBELLISHMENTS

After three years of manufacture the porcelain line was discontinued. In 1833, the company name was changed to The American Pottery Company. One of the novelties manufactured then was the hound-handle pitcher. The sides of these pitchers bore hunting scenes in relief and the handle represented a crouching hound with his nose on the rim of the top. This was an adaptation of a favorite English model and was designed by Daniel Greatback, who came here from England in 1836. In 1839, the transfer printing process was introduced and was similar also to the English method.

At East Liverpool, Ohio, in 1840, an Englishman, James Bennett, established a small pottery making earthenware, and later he added Rockingham. This industry was the beginning of the great pottery manufacturing center of to-day in Ohio.

Connecticut also had a number of small early potteries. Stoneware and lead-glazed red ware were made in Norwalk as early as 1780. Nathanial Seymour used Connecticut clay and lead glaze for stoneware household utensils, crudely decorated with designs in colors made from cobalt, verdi-

HOUND-HANDLE PITCHER

gris or manganese. Potteries were in operation in both Norwich and Stonington some time before 1800.

For many years the clay from South Amboy was sent to kilns in other sections of the country, and it was not until 1807 that Warne and Letts opened the first pottery in South Amboy. They marked their wares, which is the only way we can tell them from the pottery of John Hancock. Hancock came from England and in 1810 opened a factory at South Amboy, devoted to the manufacture of yellow ware and stoneware.

That Holland was interested in establishing a pottery in New Amsterdam at an early date was shown by the fact that the Dutch East India Trading Company sent to New Amsterdam in 1645 Jan Van Arsdale, from whom the author is descended, to ascertain whether it was practicable to establish a pottery in the new country. Later such a business was opened in the city but no records seem to exist that give specific information concerning its output.

Very little pottery was produced in New England before the Revolution. What few pieces were made were of the simplest design and served the most urgent need. After the colonies became free there was a greater incentive to manufacture for home consumption and a number of small potteries sprang up. Many of the potters were engaged in other professions and turned only their spare moments to the making of a few dishes and jars. The first kilns used did not involve any great expenditure of money but turned out an amazing variety of household utensils. Pieces from early kilns were made of the red clay, with more or less slip decoration and lead glazed. In nearly every known instance they were unsigned, though the stoneware pieces were salt glazed and in most cases bore the signature of their maker. Nearly all New England pottery of early date shows an un-

EXAMPLES OF BENNINGTON POTTERY

mistakable English influence and often was of exceptionally good color and glaze.

In 1785, Captain John Norton moved with his family from Connecticut to Bennington, Vermont, and like all his neighbors, undertook farming on a small scale. In 1893, he laid the foundation of a pottery on his farm at Old Bennington. There was a great need for simple household utensils in the near-by homes of the land-poor settlers, and the distance to com-

BENNINGTON FLINT-ENAMEL WARE

mercial centers made the cost of transportation prohibitive. Norton made at first only the ordinary type of earthenware utensils: plates, platters, jugs, and jars. This red earthenware was superseded by stoneware. In 1823, Captain Norton retired from active business and his sons Luman and John succeeded him. Until the dissolution of the firm in 1828 the stoneware was marked, "Norton & Company." This is supposed to have been the first mark used by the Norton potteries.

A new and larger pottery was built in 1833 at East Bennington by Luman Norton and his son Julius, who in 1841 held entire control of the works. Apparently he was not satisfied to make red clay and stoneware solely and began the manufacture of yellow ware and Rockingham. The latter is the yellow ware spattered with brown clay before it is fired, to give a mottled appearance.

In 1844, the firm of Norton and Fenton was formed. Christopher Webber Fenton had operated a pottery at Dorset, Vermont, before coming to Bennington. Here he married a sister of Norton's and was later taken into his business. The stoneware and Rockingham pieces made during this period were signed "Norton & Fenton, East Bennington, Vermont"; "Norton & Fenton, Bennington, Vermont," or sometimes just "Norton & Fenton."

BENNINGTON PARIAN WARE

With the closing of the Hemphill works in Philadelphia in 1837 the making of porcelain had been discontinued in this country. In 1843, it was revived in Bennington, and for a few years was made in small quantities. In 1845, the factory burned and it was not until two years later that the manufacture of porcelain could be resumed. Much of this ware was of uneven quality and without glazing. Kaolin and feldspar were both found near at hand in large quantities. Parian was made as early as 1842 and was used in the manufacture of statuary. It was an especially prepared hard-paste unglazed porcelain which resembled marble in texture. For its original purpose it was admirable but when used for household utensils its beauty was lost.

In 1849, Fenton obtained from the United States Government a patent for the process of applying colors to enamel wares. Fenton or flint enamels, as they were called, were mottled yellow and olive-green, yellow and black, yellow, brown, green, dark red, and a very little blue.

The hound-handle pitcher designed for the Bennington pottery by Daniel Greatback differed slightly from the one he made at the Jersey City pottery. In the Bennington pitcher the nose of the hound is not as near the top edge of the rim and slight variations appear in the collar that is on the dog. The actual ware was much finer and generally brown, although it was sometimes made in green or blue glaze. The branch-handle and tulip-design pitchers are unusually charming and much sought after to-day. The cow creamer, lion with its paw on a ball, the coachman and deer, are all well-known designs of Greatback. The common poodle with a basket in his mouth seems to have been designed by someone other than Greatback.

The fact that molds were made by certain firms and sold to anyone who desired to buy them makes it very hard for us to distinguish and classify unmarked pieces of pottery. As workers left one factory and went to another they carried into their new work certain characteristics of the old, with the result that styles and methods become so intermingled that it is practically impossible for us to determine their origin. Occasionally when a firm discontinued business the machinery and molds were sold to another firm, with similar results. This happened in the case of Abraham Miller, who purchased the equipment used by Hemphill when Thomas Tucker closed the business. The potter's wheel was used in some manufactories, but the majority of them depended upon the molds made of plaster of Paris.

STONEWARE JUG

CHAPTER XI

PEWTER AND SILVER

PEWTER in itself has little intrinsic value, tin and lead being the principal ingredients, with a bit of copper or antimony added. The greater the amount of tin used the more silvery the pewter appears. In most of the finer pieces we find as much as 90 per cent. tin and in the poorer less than 75 per cent. An excess of lead gave a dark, dull look to the surface and being malleable, the piece bent and dented easily.

Good pewter is smooth to the touch and has a peculiar dark tone, something between silver and lead, and can be polished to a subdued luster that is different from that of other metals and really very charming.

Pewter was used by the Chinese more than two thousand years ago, and the Japanese have known the process of making it for more than one thousand years. The Romans brought tin from the English mines and some of the early Roman official seals were of pewter. France and England used pewter in the Eleventh Century and it was in quite general use in all the European countries in the Fifteenth Century.

209

The early settlers brought very little pewter with them, but soon found need of it, and among the first things asked for from the mother country were pewter bottles. Wood was used for flat tableware. During the Seventeenth and Eighteenth centuries the colonists used a great deal of pewter, for even the wealthy did not always have silver and fine china suitable for everyday use. Between the years 1750 and 1770 much pewter was made, but like the silver a great deal of it went into the melting pot during the Revolutionary War.

For everyday household utensils pewter has long since been discarded. White metal, nickel and plated silver have taken its place and it now remains for the collector to treasure the really good pieces. The very nature of the metal caused it to wear out, and if the owner did not have it remade it was sold to the junkman or, during the early wars, made into bullets.

Most of the early pewter was imported from Europe, with Boston, New York, and Philadelphia as the distributing centers. There is a record, however, of one pewterer working in Boston years before we find mention of the first silversmith.

It was not long before the pewterers of these cities began to turn out splendid work. Possibly they had less variety in patterns than their fellow craftsmen across the ocean, yet their work suited the local demand and could be easily fashioned to suit the choice of the individual purchaser.

There were two methods of making pewter, hammering by hand or casting in molds. At times a combination of the two was used. The finishing was in general carefully done by hand, but a lathe was often used also. In making a plate a piece of metal was rolled out and then hammered into shape, this hammering giving the metal a firm and hard surface. In making larger articles such as lamps, pitchers, and teapots a mold was used. The pieces were cast in sections and soldered together.

By 1825 the china plate had almost entirely replaced pewter. A feeling of prosperity had swept in, and better and more fashionable household things were in demand. Commerce had increased and regular trade was carried on with England and other European countries. England as well as France sent the colonies fine china and porcelain which we can easily understand took the place of pewter. Yet we find that pewter candlesticks and whale-oil lamps were made until the latter half of the Nineteenth Century.

It would seem as if the trade of the pewterer was not a very lucrative one, for in so many cases we find it combined with other forms of business, such as blacksmithing or clockmaking.

The average size of plates was eight inches, although they varied from six and a quarter to twenty inches. This latter size was exceptional. Thirteen inches was ordinarily the largest size. Mixing bowls and serving dishes were from six and one half inches in diameter to the rare twelve-inch ones.

The earlier marks, though not typically English, showed a strong English influence, but after the Revolutionary War the marks became more individual in style. In Massachusetts and Rhode Island the state coat of arms was used at times.

About 1790 we find the eagle preferred by some makers, but after the first quarter of the Nineteenth Century the marks became more standardized and often the name or name and address was used as an identification.

The handle of the porringer was its weakest point, and, like the spoon, could not stand hard usage, so it was soon that pewter was replaced as material for this type of dish. Old tankards and mugs have not survived in

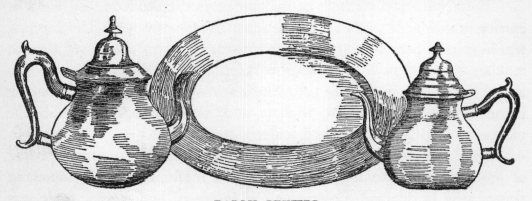

EARLY PEWTER

large numbers and we find that nearly all of the pewter communion vessels were made comparatively later.

One of the earliest colonial pewterers whose mark is still in existence is Thomas Danforth, who lived from 1703 to 1786. His work was varied for he made tea- and coffee-pots, lamps and candlesticks, to say nothing of flatware such as plates and dishes. He worked at Taunton, Massachusetts, and at Norwich, Connecticut. His pieces show skilled craftsmanship and are treasured by collectors.

Boston had Nathaniel Austen, who was famous in his trade in the latter half of the Eighteenth Century and who produced many fine examples of metalware.

In 1743, John Holden put out advertisements crying his wares, pewter utensils, hollow and flatware. It was in Market Slip, New York, that his business was established

EXAMPLES OF EARLY SILVERWARE

and grew till it won him quite a fortune for that time.

Francis Bassett, whose name is found in the 1786 directory of New York, was listed as a pewterer. At that time there were in New York Robert Byle, William Bradford, Henry Will, and Malcolm McEwen, each of whom deserves consideration. The Philadelphia City Directory of 1785 boasted of Colonel William Will as the outstanding pewterer of the city.

As we enter the second quarter of the Nineteenth Century the pewterer's trade seems to disappear and its members proudly showed Britannia ware of the newest patterns. This created a splendid market and they lost their identity as pewter makers.

It seems natural to think of the Southern colonies, with their large plantations, whose owners held to the customs and traditions of the mother country, as being the first to have any great amount of silver. The wealthier life, to which many of the Southern settlers had been accustomed, called for the

EXAMPLES OF EARLY SILVERWARE

PEWTER SHIP'S LIGHT

luxuries of the day and it was almost certain that in coming to a new country they would bring with them as many of their treasures as they possibly could. A considerable amount of English plate was to be found in Maryland, Virginia, the Carolinas, and Georgia in the early days, for it was not until late in the Eighteenth Century that American silver was made there to any extent. There were few cities and the opportunities to develop the craft of the silversmith were not as great as in the Northern colonies, consequently nearly all the pieces were imported from England. Standish Barry of Baltimore was one of the best known of the early Southern silversmiths. He followed the English design but his craftsmanship did not equal that of his contemporaries in New York or Boston.

Early American or "Colonial" silver was a modification of the styles then in use in England (*Greek*) and in France (*Roman*). It was made in a period when ideas of form, proportion, and construction were carefully given material expression. There was a logical reason for every line and curve, and any ornamentation was the result of a need for such a thing in a particular place rather than simply a means of displaying the craftsman's skill. The earlier work was not as artistic or of as fine workmanship as that of Europe; nevertheless, it had a feeling of dignity and solidity that was in keeping with the life of the new country.

Boston was the commercial center of the colonies and immense sums of money, especially Spanish coin, found their way to this port. The very inadequate banking facilities and the fluctuation of the English shilling created a desire on the part of the colonists to manufacture their surplus silver (mostly Spanish) into articles suitable for church and domestic use. This accumulation of wealth gave to the silversmiths of Boston an advantage not enjoyed by those of other places.

In the early part of the Eighteenth Century there was an abundance of silver plate, but as the necessity for funds became more pressing a portion of it found its way back to the melting pot and again became currency. The silversmiths of colonial days were not only skilled craftsmen but usually took an active part in church and civic affairs and were held in high esteem by their fellow-men.

In New England the earlier settlements were small and struggling, but when Charles I tried to rule England in a way to suit himself more than twenty thousand persons came to this country, settled here, and soon built up thriving communities. They were anxious to have all the comforts possible in their new homes, and had money enough to import many things, but they patronized the local craftsmen as well.

The first silversmith of prominence in Boston was John Hull, who came from England in 1635. Because of the scarcity of English currency for local trade the General Court of Massachusetts, in defiance of the Crown, in 1652 decided to coin shillings and the fractions thereof. These were called the "pine-tree" shillings and weighed three pennyweight. The

PAUL REVERE TEA URN AND TEAPOTS

die for this coin was made by Joseph Jenks of Lynn, Massachusetts. Hull was appointed mint master and for his services received one shilling out of every twenty. He was also financially interested in trade with the West Indies, acquired a large fortune, and was very active in public affairs. He was highly respected by all. He had as a partner Robert Sanderson, and continued to do business until his death in 1683. Some fine pieces of silver still exist marked with these two names.

Jeremiah Dummer (1645-1718) had been as a youth apprenticed to

PAUL REVERE TEA SET

Hull and acquired much of the technique of his master. One of the distinctive forms of decoration used so frequently by him is the fluted band with a plain surface. This appears to advantage on tankards and standing cups.

His brother-in-law, John Cony (1655–1722), also became a leading silversmith and because of his skill as an engraver was chosen to make the plates for the first paper money issued in the American colonies.

Edward Winslow (1669–1753) produced pieces of such fine quality as to rank him one, if not the greatest, of the earlier craftsmen.

Later we have the Reveres, father and son. Apollus Revoir (1702–1754) was born in France and came to Boston in 1715. He served his apprenticeship under John Cony. In 1723, he started in business for himself and changed his name to Paul Revere. His son Paul (1735–1818) was the third oldest of twelve children. He learned the craft from his father, who

Paul Revere
and
Son

John Coney

John Coney

Paul Revere

John Burt

Benj. Burt

EXAMPLES OF EARLY SILVERWARE

not only taught him to be a silversmith, but an expert engraver as well. He was only nineteen when his father died and he was forced to start out for himself. The plate for the first national paper currency was engraved by him in 1775. He was a patriot and a soldier as well as Boston's most famous silversmith. The Paul Revere mark was used by both father and son.

Newport was the center of the silversmith's art in Rhode Island and Samuel Vernon (1683–1737) was the first maker of note. Later, in Providence, Jabez Gorham laid the foundation of a business which his descendants have carried on.

Connecticut, being an agricultural colony, could not boast of great wealth so that the silversmith frequently had to follow some other line of business as well. The large amount of silver found in the churches would tend to show that it was ordered from Boston or New York. Cornelius Kierstede went from New York to New Haven about 1722. He was a skillful craftsman and his work shows a blending of Dutch and English influence.

The conditions in New Netherlands were quite different from those in New England as far as the silver craft was concerned. The Dutch established settlements primarily as trading posts and although they soon learned colonization was necessary, they did very little to assist the early

EXAMPLES OF EARLY SILVERWARE

settlers. It was not until 1650 that the colony began to increase to any extent. Trading had been carried on through the Dutch West India Company, exchanging furs and raw materials for the manufactured goods of Holland. For this reason there was a scarcity of the prosperous middle class compared with the number in New England and that class was the one that would most naturally buy locally. The wealthy usually imported most, if not all, of their luxuries. When the English acquired New Netherlands from the Dutch in 1664, New Amsterdam had a population of less than three thousand five hundred. Although the name was changed to New York, the Dutch customs and traditions prevailed, as was clearly shown in the silver made there.

The Seventeenth Century silver was purely Dutch in design but by the latter part of the Eighteenth Century we find the English influence had crept in. The early pieces were simple in design and beautifully executed, with a considerable amount of engraving and ornamentation. The shape and design were always appropriate to the metal used and to the use for which the piece was intended. The pieces were more massive and the silver thicker than in those of New England, but there was less refinement of line and artistic finish.

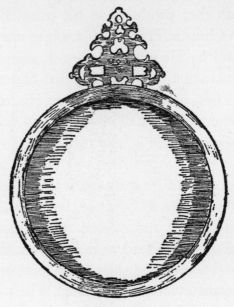

JOHN CONEY

One of the earliest of New Amsterdam's silversmiths was Jacob Boelin (1654–1729) who came from Holland to New Amsterdam about 1659. Peter Van Dyke, with his wonderful genius, was considered one of the finest silversmiths of colonial times. He was born in New York in 1684 and was actively interested in political affairs. His son Richard was also a craftsman of note. About 1690 a number of French Protestants seeking refuge from religious persecution settled in New York and among them were skillful silversmiths like Bartholomew le Roux, the father-in-law of Peter Van Dyke. These men must have unconsciously introduced a certain amount of the French technique into their later work in the colonies.

Pennsylvania was founded in 1682 by English Quakers under the able leadership of William Penn and from the start it was a prosperous colony. Philadelphia was a commercial center and until well into the Nineteenth Century was the largest city in the country. The silversmiths were offered ample opportunity to display their skill. In design, Pennsylvania silver differs very little from that produced in the other English colonies. The alms-basin in Christ's Church, Philadelphia, is the work of Cesar Chieselin, one of the first silversmiths. He was a Huguenot, going first to England and finally coming to Philadelphia, where he died about 1733. Philip Syng (1676–1739) was another silversmith of note. His son, Philip Syng, Jr. (1703–1789), made the inkstand used when our forefathers signed the Declaration of Independence. It is now to be seen in Independence Hall, Philadelphia.

Pure silver, on account of its softness, was alloyed with other metals, copper being the one to harden it. Most of the early silver plate was made from coin, which was melted and refined to the desired standard. The colonies had no established standard as in England; the early silversmiths were considered honorable men and their name or mark stamped on a piece was accepted as sufficient evidence of quality. Their method of attaining a desired standard was to rub a piece of the refined silver on a touchstone and then to compare the color of the mark or touch with that made by silver of a known quality. The next step was to pour the molten mass into shallow rectangular pans. When these pieces were cold they were ready to be rolled or hammered into sheets of any thickness required. The more silver is hammered the harder and more brittle it becomes, so to prevent it from cracking it was necessary to heat it from time to time by means of a charcoal fire. This would keep the silver in a workable condition. The peculiar bluish-gray color almost always found on old silver came from a combination of oxygen in the heated air and the copper in the alloy. We do not find this copper oxide on the present-day silver, for the modern method of polishing or buffing silver removes it entirely. In making hollow ware the metal was rolled into thin sheets and beaten with a mallet of wood or metal into desired shapes on blocks or anvils. After this the surface decorations, engraving, chasing, piercing, or repoussé work could be added. Practically all the early beakers, tankards, and cups were made in this manner.

Among the earliest pieces we find the beaker. These tall cups were

PAUL REVERE

made both for church and domestic use. They were usually engraved with symbolic figures, floral scrolls, festoons, or birds, and had a strong molding at the base. At the time of the Reformation the chalice was replaced by the beaker in the Protestant churches in Holland and naturally the Dutch colonists followed this custom in New Netherlands, and this no doubt accounts for the many beakers found in the churches here. In New England we find that besides the beaker, tankards, chalices, and candle-cups were used for communion services.

The beaker of New Netherlands was about seven inches tall, flat on the bottom. It flared slightly at the top and tapered toward the bottom. There was a heavy torus molding at the base, above which was a cut-work foliate border or a spiral wire or an ornamental band. The lip was usually engraved in designs using scrolls, strapwork, and sometimes medallions. The early type New England beaker was smaller and plainer, with straight sides, flat on the bottom and generally without a molding. Later they were taller, but still plain, with a molding on the base. The straight sides were followed by those slightly bulbous and after this style came that of straight sides and a molded band at the top and base.

The tankard of the Seventeenth Century had a slightly tapering body, broad flat base, flat-hinged lid, and heavy handle. Those made by the New

PAUL REVERE TEA SET

Netherlands silversmiths were of generous proportions, almost always cylindrical in shape. The flat lid was usually embossed or engraved, the handles ornamented and tipped with designs more or less elaborate. The foliate border above the base molding and corkscrew thumb piece were very characteristic.

The New England type of tankard up to the first part of the Eighteenth Century was comparatively low and broad and had a flat lid; then we find a simply designed finial added to a domed lid. This was followed in turn by molded finial, the design of which follows closely those used on furniture at that period. The flame and pine cone were very popular and the molded band around the body and the domed lid are typically New England.

It was not until after 1700 that we find the colonial silversmith making tea-, coffee-, and chocolate-pots. Originally they were small, these beverages being too expensive to use in quantity. During the Eighteenth Century these commodities became cheaper and the size of the pots increased accordingly. In general outline the tea- and coffee-pots were similar, in size the coffee-pot was the larger. The chocolate-pot had a straighter spout with the handle at right angles to it, a tapering body, and high domed lid. Later the handle was changed to the side opposite the spout. The early Eighteenth Century New England teapots were of two types, one round, with flat lid and splayed molded base, "S"-shaped spout, and "C"-shaped wooden handle; and the other, bell shaped, with domed lid, the base flat with a small molding, short "S"-shaped spout, and curved wooden handle with thumb piece.

The New York teapots were somewhat different in appearance, the lower part of the bulbous body was flatter and the neck narrowed and longer. Molded bands defined the contour of the body and the doomed lid. Engraving on the body and the spiral wire and pattern border at the base are typical.

By the middle of the Eighteenth Century we find the shapes have changed and the body of the teapot resembles an inverted pear. There is a slight "S" curve in the decorated spout, which projects well away from the body. The foot is molded and splayed and the lid small, slightly rounded, and topped by a finial.

The decorations by this time were showing less of the rococo influence apparent between 1740 and 1775, and were more classical in feeling. Bands of reeding and beaded moldings, engraved festoons of flowers, rosettes, oval medallions, and "bright cut" designs were popular.

The oval-shaped teapots had straight or slightly curved sides and there was no molding around the top or the flat base. Often there was a small tray with feet for the pot to rest upon. The spout was straight and the lid was either flat, slightly belled, or concave with a finial of silver, ivory, wood, or bone.

During the early part of the Nineteenth Century the French influence shows itself in the silver, particularly in the hollow ware. The pieces were

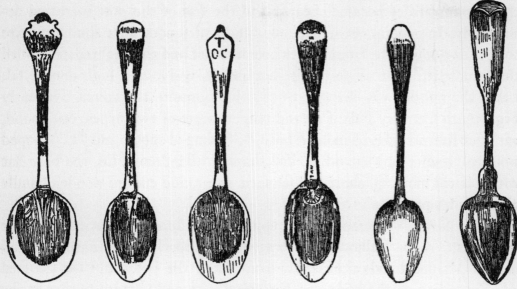

GROUP OF CHARACTERISTIC EARLY SPOONS

of thinner silver and larger in size and many were on ball feet. About 1800 a pierced railing on the tea- and coffee-pots and also sugar bowls marks the silver of Philadelphia make.

Porringers seem to have been among the most useful pieces of household ware. They were used for both solid and liquid food, and were between five and six inches in diameter and about two inches deep with a handle set nearly flush with the rim. These handles were flat and afforded the silversmiths an opportunity to show their ability in decoration. The flat open-work designs of a geometric or keyhole type were the most popular.

Forks were scarce in the early colonial times, but became quite common in the Eighteenth Century. Some were all silver and others had silver handles only, with prongs of steel. The handles were usually of the same shape and design as the spoons. Sauce-boats, creamers, salt cellars, and braziers of the Eighteenth Century were generally set on three legs, which ended in a scroll or hoof.

Spoons are probably the earliest of the domestic utensils. During the Seventeenth Century the spoon had undergone several changes, so by 1660 we find the bowl becoming oval, the stem flatter and thinner with a notched or trifid end. The bowl and stem were joined by a long plain tongue, often called a "rat-tail," which was frequently bordered by a design. In the Eighteenth Century the end of the handle was rounded and turned in the same direction as the bowl. There was a sharp ridge on the front of the rounded stem near the end. Following the rat-tail, there was the double drop on the bowl. Then the end of the stem was turned down and the ridge became very faint. The double drop on the bowl was superseded by the single drop, and such ornaments as a scroll, bird, and shell. The fiddle handle was popular about 1810. The bowl had a pointed tip and there was a broad shoulder above the bowl and on the stem where it widens.

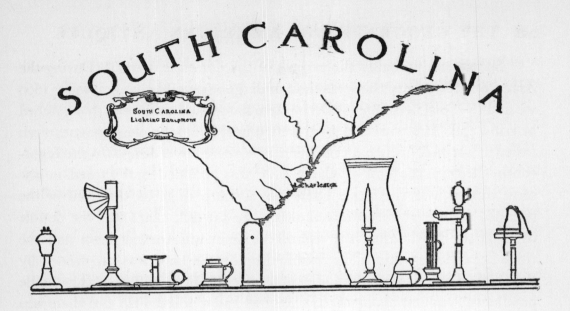

CHAPTER XII

LIGHTING EQUIPMENT[1]

WHEN the early settlers came to this country, we find them using a lamp which in design and construction was identical with those that were used in the ancient cities of Rome, Athens, and Carthage. This light was called by our forefathers the "betty" lamp and consisted of nothing more than a boat-shaped iron vessel with an open wick. Fish oil was used in it and gave but a faint glimmering light and poured forth a dense, rank-smelling smoke.

It is one of those curious anomalies that abound in history, that civilization, improving every department of daily life as well as the arts and sciences, should be content for more than eight thousand years with a lamp that was far from serviceable in the light that it gave and that had the added weakness of an unavoidable and unpleasant odor; and then with

[1]In the remote sections of South Carolina it is not unusual to find in use to-day, in the Negro cabins and in the homes of the poorer whites, oil-burning lamps similar to the earliest forms used in this country. And so I have assigned to South Carolina the chapter on early lighting equipment.

229

a sudden spurt in the short space of two hundred and fifty years should carry lighting to the advanced stage that we enjoy to-day.

The progress is even more startling when we consider that these "betty" lamps with candlewood torches constituted the sole means of light for a long period of years in the poor homes and the great homes of early America. We know that the "betty" formed the only light used aboard the *Mayflower* but that when the colony was settled ashore candlewood, so easily obtained, replaced the lamp at times. This candlewood was a resinous pitch pine cut into strips about the size of a candle and placed in holders or stuck between the stones of a fireplace. The pitch gave a very bright flame and burned freely, thereby causing considerable black smoke. It can readily be understood that the wealthier settlers had metal equipment to hold the pitch or rush, and the poorer classes depended upon ingenuity to supply these needs. It is recorded in 1630 that a small deposit of bog iron was discovered at Saugus about ten miles from Boston and that this metal was used in making household utensils and farming and carpentry equipment. There is little doubt that some of this iron went into the making of lamps.

The actual construction of the small "betty" lamp changed little through the years. The bodies were made of cast or wrought iron in one solid piece with a projecting spout in which the wick was placed. At the opposite end a curved handle was added. To this handle was attached by chain a short pick used in loosening the wick when it became embedded in grime. In some of the "betty" lamps a hooked spindle was also attached to this chain and was used to hang the lamp on a convenient peg or chair back. In other sections of the country the lamp became an integral part of a stand that could be adjusted to various heights, and still others were set into holders fashioned to receive them. The oil for the "betty" lamps was easily obtained from the small fish that swarmed the adjacent waters and when whaling became popular, fuel was obtained from this source. In time the vessels of these lamps became larger and we find double "bettys"

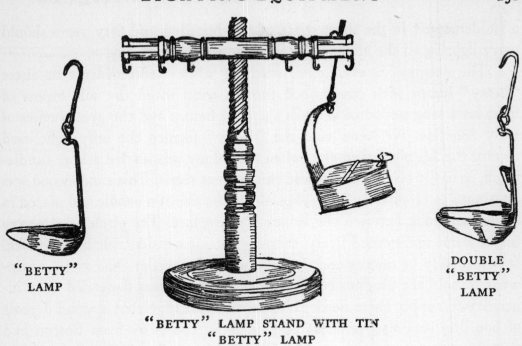

"BETTY" LAMP

"BETTY" LAMP STAND WITH TIN
"BETTY" LAMP

DOUBLE
"BETTY"
LAMP

hanging from a common staple. Although iron and tin were more commonly used in making them, a few exist that were made of pottery without covers. In general, the shape of all "bettys" was elliptical, with one end drawn out to form the spout into which the wick was laid. At the opposite end was attached a crudely wrought handle in which at the top was set the chain carrying the small pick and spindle. The early examples usually have no covers, but in the later iron lamps a flat piece of metal, pronged at the front end to pass around the wick, was attached to a pivot at the back and slid sideways across the vessel. The lids on tin lamps were hinged and raised off the reservoir instead of sliding. Iron "bettys" were superseded by lamps of tin and pewter.

A remarkable device for economy appeared in some of the lamps. A small gutter ran beneath the wick spout proper and as the drippings ran over the spout they were caught by the under gutter and carried into the vessel to be used again. As the wick was apt to draw more oil than could

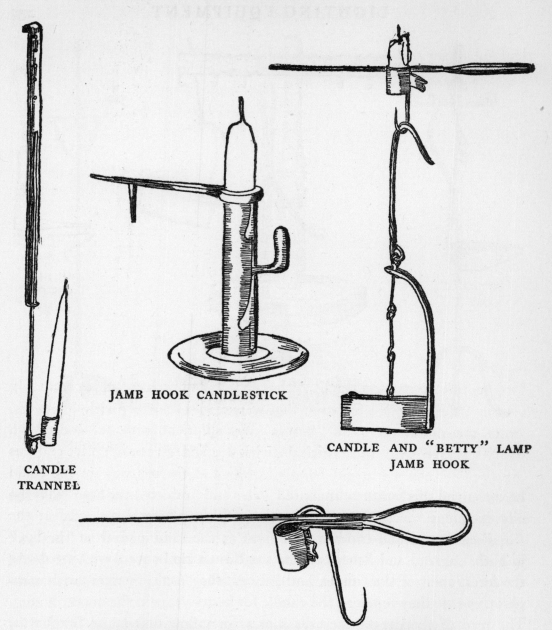

CANDLE
TRANNEL

JAMB HOOK CANDLESTICK

CANDLE AND "BETTY" LAMP
JAMB HOOK

SHOWING DETAIL OF CANDLE AND "BETTY" LAMP
JAMB HOOK

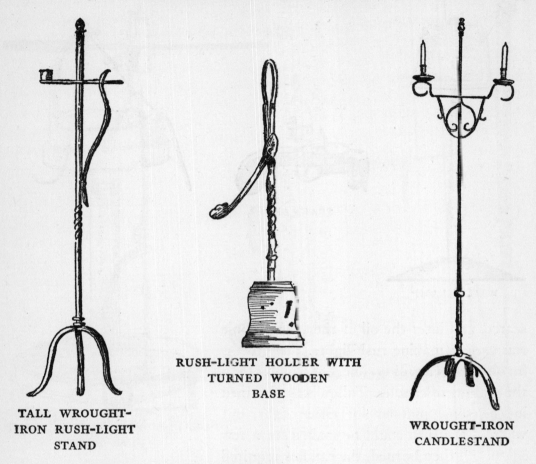

TALL WROUGHT-
IRON RUSH-LIGHT
STAND

RUSH-LIGHT HOLDER WITH
TURNED WOODEN
BASE

WROUGHT-IRON
CANDLESTAND

be consumed this feature eliminated waste and protected the floor from the oily drippings.

Rush lamps and candles were used at the same period as "bettys" in both England and America. The small rush lamps were without doubt the forerunners of the candle, and because they could be made with comparative ease they replaced the candle for many years in the poorer homes. The reed of the cat-o'-nine-tails soaked in tallow or oil and braided or "bundled" formed the rush light.

Bayberries which grew all along the coast and the fat of wild animals from the adjacent forests gave substitutes for tallow when cattle were

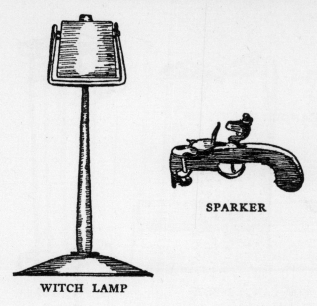

WITCH LAMP

SPARKER

TIN "BETTY" LAMP ON STAND

scarce, and later the oil of the sperm whale was used in making rush lights. The process involved was a tedious one, but simpler than the making of candles. Tallow was obtained in the same manner for either light, but whereas the rush could be soaked for a few hours and then burned, the candles required carefully made wicks and constant attention during the dipping. The holder for the rush light appeared in countless shapes and sizes of all iron, or iron and wood construction. Nevertheless, they are easily recognized from other lighting equipment, for the scissors-like prong or clip which held the rush appears on no other lighting device.

The making of candles was a complicated and varied task. What was considered the best wax was made of equal parts of sheep and ox tallow. Fat from the hog was never used, for it gave when burning a most disagreeable odor and dripped and ran more than any other fat. Vegetable-oil

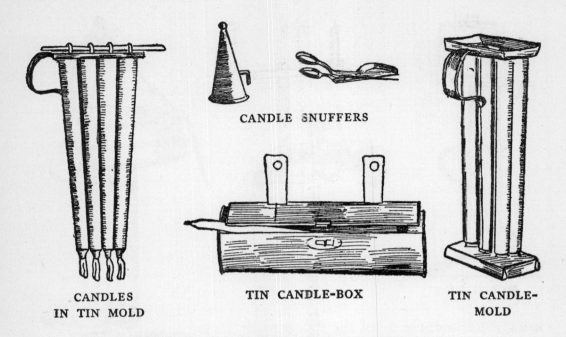

CANDLE SNUFFERS

CANDLES
IN TIN MOLD

TIN CANDLE-BOX

TIN CANDLE-
MOLD

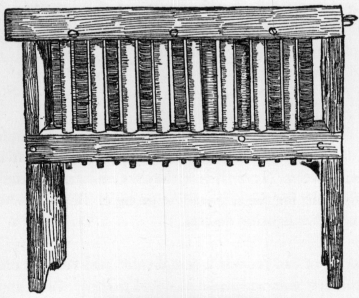

POTTERY CANDLE-MOLD

235

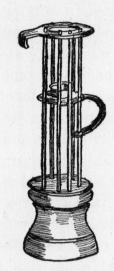

A WROUGHT-IRON
CANDLESTICK ON
WOODEN BASE

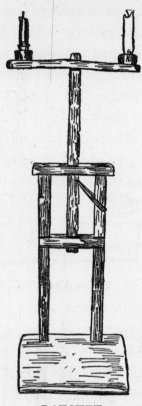

RATCHET
CANDLESTAND

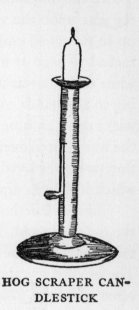

HOG SCRAPER CAN-
DLESTICK

substitutes were great favorites, particularly that of the bayberry, for it gave off a pungent woody odor that was not unpleasant. After the tallow blocks were made they were cut into small scraps that could be quickly melted without burning when placed over heat. The wax when soft was put into a pot of hot water and as the grease came to the top it was skimmed off. In this way the impurities in the fat were left in the water at each skimming. This process was repeated a number of times to insure greater refinement and the tallow was then strained through a horsehair cloth to remove the particles of dirt that had been missed in the skimming.

Wicks of small bits of cotton or twisted linen had been previously prepared and the wax was worked with the hands about these wicks. To keep it soft and workable it was dipped repeatedly into hot water. In working the wax upon the wick the small pieces were wrapped from the large end up to the small end of the candle. The string of the wick was usually attached to pegs or nails along the wall in order that it might be kept taut while the wax was applied. Oil was used to prevent the tallow from adhering to the hands. A quicker method of making candles was to fasten the wicks upon an iron or wooden ring which was suspended over a kettle and the wax poured over them until they were the desired size. While still warm they were removed from the iron and rolled between two small paddles which had been dipped in hot water to prevent adhesion.

The last method and the one with which we are most familiar involved the use of a mold. These molds were made of tin, pewter, brass, and pottery, ranging from single candles to as many as three dozen in one mold. The process was simpler but required skill to keep the wicks taut and centered while the tallow was poured in. A single piece of wick was run from one hole into the next through the entire mold. Small branches or pieces of wood were inserted across the bottom to hold the strings as nearly as possible in the center. Hot wax was then poured into each opening. When the mold was cold the wick was cut at top and bottom and the whole mold plunged for a second into boiling water. This tended to loosen the wax from the sides and with little effort the candles could be pulled from the top.

For many years candles remained a luxury and were only used for special occasions. It is recorded in 1634 that they sold for as much as four pence each. As time passes, itinerant candlemakers appear, going from town to town and house to house, making a year's supply of candles from the materials that the housewife had saved.

So much for candlemaking. Let us look at the various candleholders that appeared. The most primitive consisted of a simple spike in upright position upon a broad base and was known as a "pricket." Needless to say, the candle invariably split when the spike was pushed into it and soon it was discovered that a holder was more practical. These fixtures were usually made of iron by a blacksmith and devised in a brutal fashion. Later the more graceful tall wrought-iron candlestick appeared. These holders consisted of a tall shaft with a cross arm upon which the candle-holders were placed at one or both ends. The arm itself was straight and flat and ended in many cases in a decorative scroll which supported the saucers of the holder. Sometimes the supports are scrolled as well. These supports or braces were so constructed that the arm could be raised to various heights on the shaft. On many candleholders of this type we find the shaft supported by three pedestal legs, and on others the shaft runs directly into a wooden block which serves as a base. Wooden candlestands were often used in the outlying districts because they could be easily made at home, in the absence of an ironworker in the immediate neighborhood. They exist in varied forms, but usually had a threaded center shaft upon which a broad arm could be screwed to various heights. The base consisted of two flat crossed feet, a small block, or tripod legs set into a platform. The thick arms were hollowed out at either end to receive the candles. On the more finished examples we find that a round shelf was set over the center shaft and the stand then served as a small table as well. A simpler type was the ratchet stand with a base usually of a solid block of wood into which two upright shafts were set with a ratchet between which ad-

TYPICAL CANDLESTICKS OF GLASS, POTTERY, AND BRASS

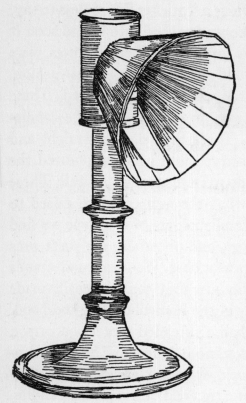

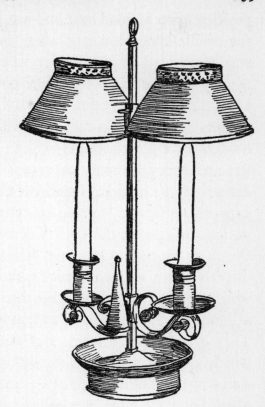

BRASS CANDLESTICK WITH
METAL SHADE

DOUBLE CANDLESTAND WITH
METAL SHADE AND
WEIGHTED BASE

justed the height of the candle. Different sections of the country introduced variations into the candlestands, the classification of which is practically impossible.

The earliest candlesticks consisted of nothing more than a flat tin or iron base with a round neck to hold the candle. A small adjuster set into a slot in the side appeared in the taller examples and served to raise the candle as it burned down. Three or four small notches in the side of the slot held the adjuster at the desired height. One variety of these holders is known through New England as the "hog scraper." It was made of iron with a slight lip projecting near the top and terminated in a circular convex base. It received its rather indelicate name because it was used to remove bristles from slaughtered hogs.

In the gradual improving of the candlestick a spring was placed inside the hollow shaft at its base. The candle was pressed down and held in place by a cap screwed to the top of the shaft. In the center of this cap was a small opening which allowed the wick to protrude and as the candle burned it was forced upward by the spring from beneath, keeping the wick always at the proper level.

It is only logical to find in time that metal shades appear on candlesticks. At first these shades were merely crude cylinders or flat backs of tin, but later a more shapely shade is used and often is supported by a decoratively scrolled bracket. The early student lamp is found in the form of a table candlestand with base and shades made of tin and adjustable on a center brass rod. The rod is embedded in a deep tin saucer which has been loaded with sand to counterbalance the weight of the top. Scrolled arms support the candle saucers and the pierced necks of the shades give a note of delicacy and decoration to the lamp.

Brass candlesticks of various types were known in the early days of our country but lacked, in the minds of the settlers, the elegance of Sheffield sticks. The latter are given great mention in wills and inventories and we are led to believe that they existed here in great quantities in the wealthier homes. They were in most instances exquisitely designed and ornamented and stand out in sharp contrast to the simple holders of brass and pewter. To describe the many shapes that the candlestick assumed through the years is impossible here and with the exception of those of glass, which we shall consider later, we shall leave them and turn to the always fascinating wall sconce.

The back of the sconce served two purposes, that of a reflector and to break the draft that was apt to blow out the flame. In the earlier patterns the entire sconce was made of a long flat piece of tin with a scalloped top and a base consisting of a half-round projecting platform with an upright

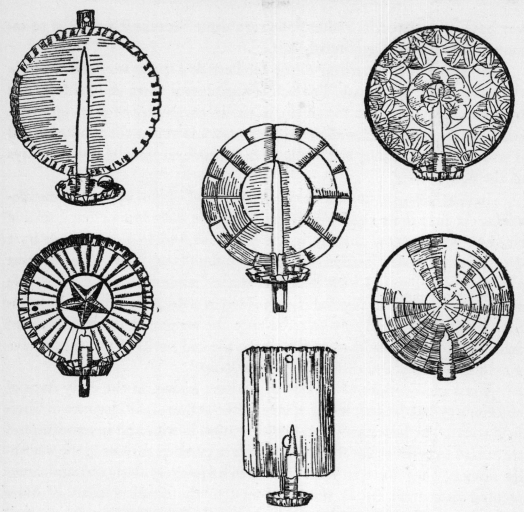

EARLY TIN, PEWTER, AND MIRROR SCONCES

border into which was set a small circular neck of tin to hold the candle. At the top a small hole through the arch made it possible to hang the sconce, and the flat base also permitted it to set upon a table. As time went on this long, narrow sconce was developed into countless forms each having the candleholder separate from the back and held securely to it at the end of a long arm or attached directly to the base of the back. They came in

SINGLE BULL'S EYE
LIGHT OF PEWTER

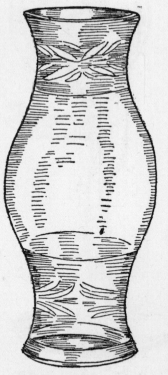

HURRICANE GLOBE

many shapes and forms: sunburst, star, pie-crust, fluted, and mirrored. In a few rare cases the reflector was made of small pieces of pewter on a tin back. Oval, elliptical, and square backs with scalloped edges and unembellished centers mark the earlier types, and other later styles are shaped and completely covered with small pieces of mirror. The author has an interesting early tin sconce with more than twenty small pieces of pewter applied to the back and sides. The edges round out half an inch from the back and a piece of glass covers the entire front face to keep the reflectors from becoming discolored.

Snuffers were devised to extinguish the flames of candles without the spattering wax and disagreeable odor that are present when they are merely blown out. They were scissors-like in construction and their action was to smother the flame when they were closed. On one of the blades was a small box into which the wick was pressed and retained after cutting. A more elaborate and rare type of which I am fortunate enough to own a splendid example has a third unit in the form of a small brush that works automatically in brushing the wick end and soot from the box. Other simple snuffers were made of thin sheets of tin in cone shape and we find that many of these were made as an integral part of elaborate holders. For candles encased in "hurricane glasses" and for the candle chandeliers above the reach an ingenious extension snuffer was devised, which extended several feet when the members were opened.

Tradition attributes to Benjamin Franklin the innovation of the double-wick theory. Franklin's father Josiah was a tallow chandler and in his shop Benjamin, at the early age of ten, began cutting wicks. His curiosity led him to experiment in freeing the lamps of soot and carbon, which dimmed the flame. Eventually he worked out the idea that two wicks placed side by side in a lamp would cause a stronger current of air and bring more oxygen in contact with the flame, thereby giving a stronger and freer light. His invention was received with much enthusiasm and the lamp makers produced as a result a new style of single lamp with double wick. These lamps afforded much better light and were practical and serviceable. If we will stop to notice, it may be easily seen that this innovation influenced whale-oil lamps as well as candle burners.

Camphine was used in many early oil lights and such lamps are easily recognized by the long wick spout which they invariably bear. There was a reason for lengthening the spout when camphene was used. The liquid was dangerous because it was extremely explosive and should a spark however small get into the oil chamber, disastrous results would follow. To keep the flame as far as possible from the contents of the reservoir, added length was

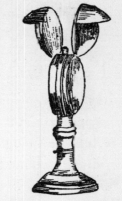

DOUBLE BULL'S-EYE LIGHT

"BETTY" LAMP WITH TIME INDICATOR

given the wick spout. Many attachments were invented for these lamps but none of them was successful and the use of camphene for lighting purposes was discarded.

Among the more interesting lamps of the period is the pewter clock light. In some respects its construction is similar to a "betty." The reservoir is supported on a tall shaft springing from a wide saucer base, the distinctive feature being that the font is of glass and resembles an inverted pear in shape. About this chamber runs a narrow band of pewter marked with the hours in Roman numerals. The font was so proportioned with regard to the figures that the oil as it burned lower marked, by its level, the hour.

A reading lamp with bull's eye lenses flanking the flame at one or two sides forms one of the most serviceable lamps of the time and without any doubt one of the most beautiful. The oil tank is drum shaped and attached to a base not unlike that of an early pewter candlestick. The English lights of this style almost without exception boast two lenses, whereas the early lamps made in this country had but one.

As we have stated elsewhere, great quantities of oil were obtained from the small fish so plentiful along the seaboard, but it was not until whaling became established as a thriving industry that the importance of oil was recognized. The sperm whale which appeared in great numbers off the coast of New England and elsewhere yielded enormous quantities of splen-

PEWTER WHALE-OIL LAMPS

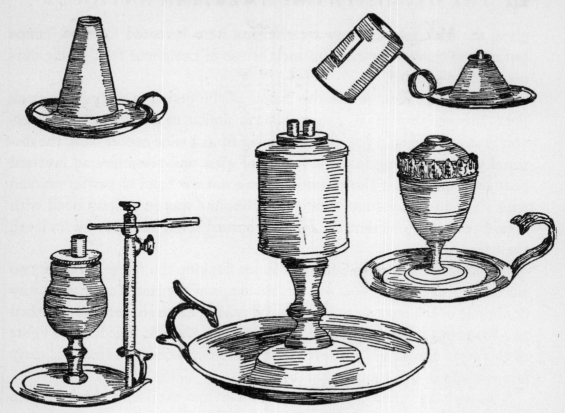

EARLY PATENT LAMPS

did illuminating oil. Formerly any whale oil was used but the ordinary kind was far inferior to that of the sperm whale, whose oil was lighter and unfortunately more costly. Before we pass on to a description of the lamps used at this period we must understand how inadequate was the open-wick lamp. What few advantages it had over the "betty" were trifling compared with the disadvantages that it still retained. A double light, to be sure, gave a more brilliant illumination but also produced a double amount of smoke and odor. In 1783, M. Argand introduced the first patent lamp and in the following decade some five hundred patents were issued on various types of whale-oil and lard lamps.

The great innovation in Argand's burner was the perforating of the

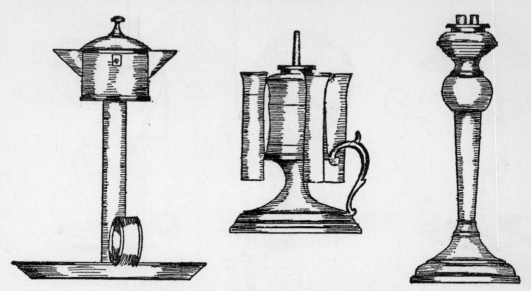

EXAMPLES OF EARLY LIGHTING EQUIPMENT

metal neck which supported the chimney with small holes through which the air was constantly drawn in against the flame. The result was a brighter, cleaner flame.

We may start our enumeration of patent lamps with the petticoat lamp, as most common. This lamp boasts a double wick and a separate filling hole at the side. In size it is very small and consists of a circular and slightly conical-shaped reservoir on a hollow conical tin base. From the bottom ring of the upper member to the bottom of the base is attached a flat half-circle handle. The actual reservoir is small and contains very little oil and hence gives a dim, flickering light. We consider this the cause of their appellation "sparking lights" and firmly believe that their insufficient light aided and abetted incipient romances. Another story has it that one was given to the guest at the taverns who had imbibed too much, because it was guaranteed to go out shortly in case the user forgot to extinguish it before falling asleep. Other tin lamps were similarly constructed

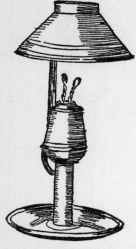

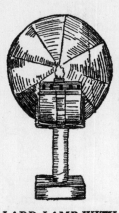

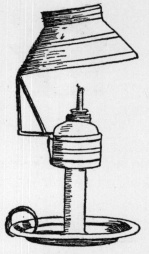

CAMPHINE LAMP
WITH METAL SHADE

LARD LAMP WITH
REFLECTOR

WHALE-OIL LAMP WITH
METAL SHADE

but the conical base was replaced with a flat saucer from the center of which rose an upright shaft that supported the actual lamp. Still others were encased in a circular tin neck, several inches in breadth, which was attached to the saucer base. A hole in the top permitted air to enter and small mica windows at the sides allowed a feeble glimmer of light to escape. A few rarer lamps had bases of pewter with glass reservoirs delicately chased, and necks and wick holders of brass. Economy led to the making of peg lights, which were little more than the lamps which we have already described with a small round base about the thickness of a candle. This base was stuck into a candlestick, which was thus converted into a lamp.

A few patent lamps were made with reflectors, and others had shades painted to match the base. The shades were usually of tin and attached to the handle by a small hinge so that they might be easily turned back when the wick was being lighted or trimmed.

Brass was never so popular a metal for lamps as it was for candlesticks, and although pewter replaced tin in many of the better lamps, the use of brass was uncommon until the middle of

the Nineteenth Century. Attempts were made to manufacture lamps of silver but they were never in common use. Price may have been responsible for their rejection, but what few examples exist seem to lack the beauty of the pewter lamps and we can see little advantage in their use. Pewter was considered better and was more expensive than tin, and consequently more time was spent in designing lamps of this metal, but some of the japanned tin lamps deserve equal comment for both beauty and serviceableness.

Lard lamps in general construction are similar to the whale-oil lights, but with larger reservoirs and broad, thick wick holders to draw the heavy oil in sufficient quantity to afford good light. They, too, had in many cases reflectors and shades and, in a few late cases, glass chimneys.

Lanterns in some form or other are closely bound to all periods of American history. The horn lantern was without doubt the earliest type used here and gave a very diffused light through its windows of scraped cow's horn. These lanterns were made of tin or iron and were circular in shape with a peaked tin top. They had four large windows on the sides, one of

which hinged to make a door. Four dormer-shaped opening windows were placed in the conical top to permit free passage of air in the body. Piecing lines across the windows were necessitated by the fact that horn could not be obtained in large pieces.

Street lighting was unknown for many years and individuals who ventured out after dark were always equipped with lantern lights of some sort. In 1690, Boston placed at the corners of all important streets iron fire baskets which were kept burning by additional fuel supplied at regular intervals by the night watchman as he made his rounds. These baskets were set on tall posts and gave forth a welcome flare to the loiterers bound homeward from the tavern or public house. A larger basket of the same type was placed on one of the high hills near the city and acted as an emergency signal in case of sudden Indian attacks, fires, or other disturbances. Really adequate lighting equipment for public highways was unknown until 1772, when John Hancock and a committee of citizens were appointed to arrange for the establishment of

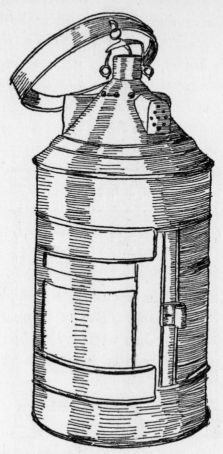

AN EARLY TIN LANTERN WITH
COW'S HORN WINDOW AND
DORMER DRAUGHTS

proper lighting posts. They sent to England for several hundred lamps and the record reads that they were to be "suitable for properly lighting ye streets and lanes of ye towne." So far as the records show, they were made with glass sides and equipped with oil reservoirs.

The watchman's lantern, usually triangular in shape, is well known to all of us. Late examples carried a bull's-eye lens and an applied wire handle at the side with which to hold it. Sometimes a red shield slid before

TIN LANTERN WITH PIERCED
BALUSTRADE AND GREEN
GLASS BULL'S-EYE
LENS

the lens, converting the lantern into a signal. A home-made example exists which has a half-round back nailed to a wooden frame in front. A groove in the wood of the frame holds a square piece of glass. These lanterns have from one to five candleholders, which lead us to suppose that they were not used during the first year of colonization but came in at a slightly later date.

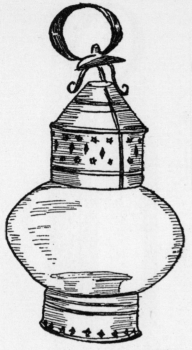

BLOWN-GLASS LANTERN

WATCHMAN'S LANTERN

The Paul Revere light has come near being extinguished by senti-
mental popularity. We can scarcely suppose in our wildest moments of
conjecturing that one of these lanterns hanging in the tower of Old North
Church could have thrown a beacon light through its tiny pierced holes to
Paul Revere "on the opposite shore," but to preserve the tradition we
will suppose that he carried such a lantern as he rode that night "through
every Middlesex village and farm." The Revere lanterns were all similar
in style and varied only in the pierced decoration that was applied to their
sides. Such motifs as the Masonic emblems, eagles, hearts, and legends concerning their ownership were most common.

Probably the most serviceable of early lanterns was the square, glass-
encased type. They often carried candles but in many cases whale-oil
lamps. Bands of metal wire around all four sides protected the glass from

EARLY RAILROAD
LANTERN

WATCHMAN'S
LANTERN

breakage yet in no way hindered the passage of light through the glass. Later examples discarded the square shape and became round and narrow. The early globes were of a bulbous shape but in time the sides were straightened and the height increased.

So on through countless variations mounting well into the hundreds we may trace this type of light. But in general they were all based on the same principles and served the same utilitarian purposes. Their great variety we may attribute to the insufficient street lighting which necessitated the carrying of lights whenever one ventured abroad after sunset. In a large family many lanterns would be needed for this service, as well as for indoor lighting, and if the family was not of means it was only logical that the home-made equipment sufficed; in this home-made class we may record most of the deviations from accepted types.

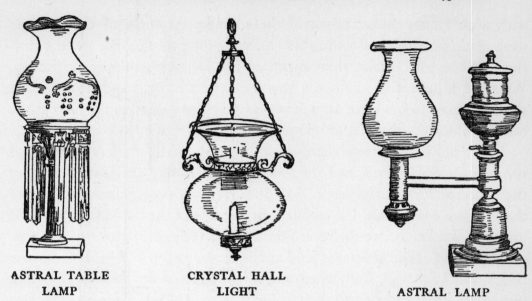

ASTRAL TABLE
LAMP

CRYSTAL HALL
LIGHT

ASTRAL LAMP

The common use of glass brought about great changes in lighting equipment and in many sections, at a comparatively early date, replaced tin, brass, and pewter. In 1750, in Quincy, Massachusetts, glass lamps and candlesticks were manufactured and some thirty years later others were made in Temple, New Hampshire. Both types were crude and of poor-quality glass, the former characterized by a peculiar twist given the upright support and the latter by the wick tubes which protruded through cork instead of the usual brass or tin. Between these years other glass lamps were put on the market, but we know little of their origin and manufacture aside from the casual mention accorded them in advertisements of glass factories. The Sandwich glass industry existed in 1825, and thereafter flooded the country with glass lamps and candlesticks of many styles. We shall not go into the actual manufacturing of these lamps, for that is covered in the chapter on glass, but suffice it to say they were beautiful and serviceable.

The early glass lamps had simple square or round bases which flared up to support a bulbous reservoir terminating in a cap of brass and pewter with wick spouts characteristic of these lamps. As some of these lamps were made for sperm oil and others for camphine we find the same variations in the wick spout that appeared in the corresponding tin lamps. When, at a later date, kerosene was used the wick spouts became much shorter. Many colors were used in making the Sandwich lamps, clear glass, canary, blue, amethyst, and opaque white being the most common.

Hanging hall lanterns were made in many of the glass factories that sprung up at this period, and the few that exist to-day are dearly loved by the collector for their grace of line and exquisite workmanship. Most of these lights were made for candles, perhaps because the filling of an oil tank at such height would be a difficult task. The glass globe which constituted most of the lamp was held at the center or top in a brass or bronze ring, ornately carved, from which ran three chains of similar metal meeting in a small plate attached to the ceiling. The base of the globe was set into a small metal neck which in the case of the oil-burning lanterns concealed the reservoir.

Many pages could be covered with descriptions of the inventions that were introduced during the early part of the Nineteenth Century. Attempts of all sorts to improve the light and shape of lamps led to a variety of results. The Argand lamp was improved by a slight change in the wick that permitted freer oil supply and thereby replaced the light sperm oil, usually used in these lamps, with the cheaper heavier whale oil. The outstanding innovation of these years was an improvement on the Argand lamp introduced by Benjamin Thompson. In order to spread the rays of light from the lamp and do away with the heavy shadows that were cast by the base he extended an arm at one or two sides of an upright shaft and placed the burner and small circular reservoir at the end. In some cases the entire oil supply was held in this reservoir while in others the reservoir was a part of the center shaft and the oil drained through the arm to the burner. These lamps were a vast improvement on the heavy base affairs that had preceded them and opportunity was given for beautiful decorative effects in both shaft and side arms. The flame was in nearly every instance shielded by a tall narrow glass shade.

The use of cut-glass prisms and pendants on some of the astral or modified Argand lamps described above gave an additional note of grace and elegance and opened a new field of decoration for candlesticks as well as for wall sconces and table lamps. When candles were no longer used as the sole source of light their decorative qualities prevented their being discarded. The mantel candelabra known as "girandoles" consisted of three parts, a centerpiece with an upright and two side arms, and two end pieces without the side arms. Their center shaft was made of openwork brass depicting favorite subjects, such as Romeo and Juliet, Babes in the Wood, Paul and Virginia, and many others. This shaft was set upon a single or double base of marble. A foliate brass crown of elliptical shape fitted over each arm and the center shafts, and from holes pierced through its edges were suspended long crystal pendants. A few brass table lamps, incorrectly called astral, had the same construction of a round brass crown above a plain or turned center upright, with the suspended drops of varying shape and size. Chandeliers of the period were made entirely of glass with a profusion of drops, pendants, and prisms. A few types were made of brass or silver with prisms suspended from the burners and hung in strings between the arms.

With our highly improved electrical lighting of to-day, we are prone to scoff at the candle and oil lights of yesterday, but with their passing went a certain glamour and charm that we can never duplicate with modern lights, however perfected.

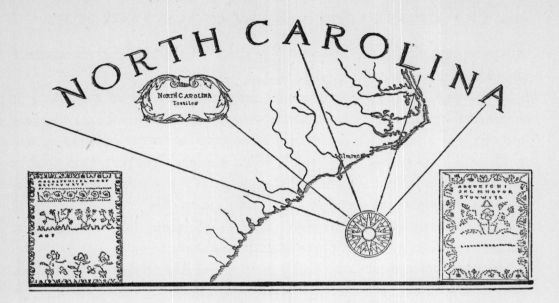

CHAPTER XIII

HOOKED RUGS, COVERLETS, AND TEXTILES[1]

JUST when and where the first American hooked rugs were made has never been determined, but it is safe to say that they were made during the Eighteenth Century. They were no doubt an attempt on the part of our thrifty pioneer women to create an article necessary for the home that would be beautiful as well as useful. In the primitive early homes the dirt floors were covered with rush. We see that this was not unusual when we recall that all the great public rooms of English homes, such as the Presence Chamber in Hardwick Hall, had rush-strewn floors, which stood out in strong contrast to the tapestry-hung walls. The lack of warmth in these floors as well as the fact that they became muddy and damp when

---

[1]In the mountain sections of North Carolina to-day are many small mountain industries where one may purchase hooked rugs and coverlets made in the homes of mountain women in the same patterns and by the same methods as their forebears used generations before them. Little has been changed, but the foresight of a few people here and there has made a profitable industry of their labors and has preserved for us one of the most charming phases of colonial life. In recognition of this fact, I have given their state this chapter on the textile industry of early times.

257

HOOKED RUG

snow or rain was tramped across them, soon led the colonists to replace them with floors of wood, covered occasionally with animal skins, this use of which may have been inspired by the Indians.

In Pennsylvania, we find wooden floors covered with sand, but in time all who could afford it bought rugs in England; the less fortunate were forced to resort to their ingenuity to produce something to take the place of this luxury. The careful, thrifty housewives, allowing nothing to go to waste, utilized the contents of the scrap bag in making a crude but much-needed floor covering.

The earliest of these rugs were little more than an overlapping of pieces of cloth sewed upon a coarse homespun background, usually linen. This served the purpose but could scarcely be called artistic. With the aid of a dye pot, narrow strips of cloth, a piece of homespun linen or sacking, and a little imagination, the first hooked rug was evolved.

The linen backing was securely fastened to a frame not unlike a small quilting frame and upon this the pattern was drawn. The narrow strips of

HOOKED RUG

material were pulled with a small hook through the coarse mesh of the foundation in loops following the design. Sometimes the loops were cut but frequently they were left just as they were hooked through. As in most primitive art, the original designs were suggested by the every-day things. Garden flowers and animals were great favorites. We find the rose in all shades of red and pink with gay large green leaves against a neutral background. There seemed to be no end to the combinations that could be introduced. Dogs, cats, rabbits, and birds often crudely drawn and out of proportion add a charming quaintness to the design.

In the seaport towns it is quite natural that we should find ships and nautical devices executed with truly wonderful results. The "Welcome" rugs carry a good old feeling of hospitality and friendliness. Geometric designs were used, though it is difficult to find one that is perfect and with regular outline. The coarsely woven fabric of the background was not the best thing upon which to draw a straight line or circle. In a random flower pattern such irregularities pass unnoticed, and we find that the great de-

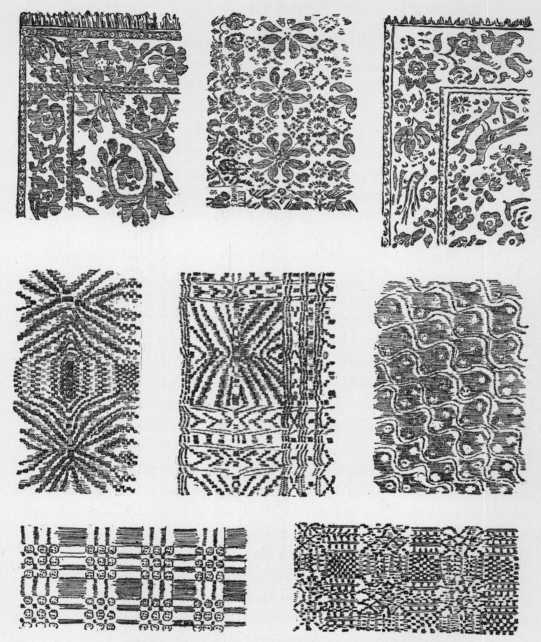

EIGHT EXAMPLES OF WOVEN COVERLETS

mand to-day of collectors of hooked rugs is for these patterns in preference to the geometric or animal designs.

The braided rug may not appeal as much as the hooked rug, although some very charming examples have been found. In these rugs the material was cut in narrow strips and braided in flat braids, the width varying more or less according to the material. The braids were then sewed together along the edges, making an oval or circular rug. When well made these rugs lie flat on the floor and retain their shape indefinitely. Sometimes several rows of braiding were put around a hooked rug for a finishing touch.

No matter what the color or design, there is always a fascination about all of these old rugs for the lover of antiques.

One of the strictly feminine crafts coming down to us from colonial days is quilt making, and we find many of the primitive methods as well as patterns still in use to-day in the remote mountain sections of North Carolina. All the hardships of pioneer days could not suppress the love of the beautiful, and the creative, home-making genius of woman found its self-expression in working out the intricate designs of these bed coverings.

Until the Nineteenth Century the bed held an important and conspicuous position as an article of furnishing. Houses had few rooms and we often find a bed in a hallway or living room. Naturally the housewife took great pride in its equipment and spent many hours on the hangings and coverings. It is to be supposed that the colonists brought some bed coverings from England though this supply must have been limited and in need of replenishing. And as they were also used to hang over doors and windows to keep out the wintry drafts we can see that many were needed in a comparatively small home.

On the large Southern plantations and in the great manor houses of the North, where entertaining was lavish, slaves were taught to weave.

Quilts, whether patched, pieced, or woven, were made in all of the colonies, and the fact that similar and even identical designs were found all over the country leads us to suppose that some of the patterns used were old and brought from England, Holland, or France.

Woven coverlets were 'given various colloquial names in different sections. They were made on a hand loom thirty inches wide in two strips of the desired length and then sewed together to make a spread. The warp was usually of white cotton or linen and the woof of colored wool. In many cases these materials were grown, spun into thread or yarn, dyed, and woven into coverlets by the housewife. Later there were professional, itinerant weavers who, traveling from house to house, used the yarn that had been made ready for them, on the looms of their patrons. Others had looms set up in their places of business. Being more broadly experienced they were able to weave more intricate patterns, such as birds, flowers, foliage, and human figures. Queer, but these coverlets never seem to have the originality of color or design that gives charm to the home-made ones. Some looms were made wide enough to receive the whole spread in one piece and these coverlets are much in demand to-day, although most of those that we find show the center seam.

The women of colonial times were most skillful in the making of vegetable dyes, and throughout the years these colors have retained their luster and brilliancy. This may have been a lesson well learned from the Indians, along with many others. Blue and red were favorites, but yellow, pink, green, and brown were added. Black runs through many of the designs. It was always necessary to use a mordant to set the dye, and alum and sometimes copperas served this purpose. Indigo made any shade of blue depending on how long the material was left in the dye. If the wool had been sunburned it turned blue-green when dipped into indigo. With cochineal all reds from rose to claret could be obtained, and when diluted the pinks resulted. The barks of the walnut, chestnut, and hickory gave a brown dye, and black oak and hickory made green. For a lovely light green

QUILTED ALL-WHITE COVERLET

the shell of the young butternut was best. Sumac, saffron, goldenrod, wild cherry, laurel, and peach leaves gave various yellows, and scrub oak, log wood, or nut galls, black. This is by no means a complete list of dyes but will serve to give an idea of the variety of materials from which dyes could be made.

In the pieced and sewn quilt we find such a variety of colors and designs that a classification is almost useless. The earliest covers were made for durability and are not as artistic as those produced when the housewife had more time to devote to their making and designing. Cotton and linen were favorite materials, no doubt because they were easily obtainable.

Silk, satin, and velvet cloths appear but were never used to any great extent.

Simplest of all the designs was the plain pieced-work cover made of small blocks five or six inches square. Each of these blocks was in turn made of smaller pieces in two or more colors. It is readily seen how practical these covers were, for the minutest scrap of material could be used in them. Some blocks were units in themselves although often a part of a large pattern, usually geometric in design. The "star" patterns are always lovely. These are made of small triangular pieces shaping a star and so arranged in color that the whole design shades from the center of the star to the edge.

JACOB'S LADDER

Patchwork quilts required more skill than those that were pieced because the design was cut out and sewed down upon a solid background of another piece of material. These motifs could be made of a solid color or of blending or contrasting colors. The background was generally white linen or unbleached muslin. For convenience they were also worked in small blocks and sewn together when the required number was finished. In addition to the top and back a third thickness of material, an interlining, was added and held to the front or back with a fine hand stitching called quilting, done on a frame made for the purpose. The quilting frame consisted of four narrow pieces of wood with

CONVENTIONAL TULIP

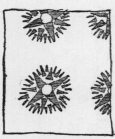

SUNBURST

WHEEL OF FORTUNE

PRINCESS FEATHERS

holes in either end of each. Two of the pieces were longer than the quilt and two shorter. Some of these frames stood on uprights about the height of a table but the majority of them were pegged at the corners to form a rectangle and placed on the backs of four chairs for support. The edges of the frame were bound with strips of cloth and to these the quilt was basted to hold it firmly. As one end of the quilting was finished the rod was detached and rolled back.

Over the lining was spread a thin layer of wool or cotton and then the pieced top. Great care was taken to keep the edges of the quilt even and the pattern was then drawn. This consisted of single, double, or triple lines running diagonally across the whole, squares, diamonds, shells, pineapples, fans, and ostrich feather designs. They were all outlined in a fine running stitch, sometimes as many as twenty stitches to the inch. It took a tremendous amount of patience and time to produce some of the marvelous quilting found in the old coverlets. Elaborate centers and corners against a background so closely quilted that it threw the pattern in relief were not uncommon. Sometimes the design was raised by stuffing it with cotton forced through the open mesh of the lining, with a sharppointed instrument resembling a needle, after the quilt was removed from the frame. We find many names of varied suggestion attached to the quilts of this time:

LOG CABIN

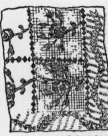

NORTH CAROLINA LILY

ROSE OF SHARON

ROSE WREATH

CHARTER OAK

"The Lincoln Platform," "The Democratic Rose," and the "Prince of Wales Feathers," are a few famous ones.

The most beautiful of all American quilts were produced in the late Eighteenth Century.

In the old wills of our earliest history we find mention of damask and turkeywork in such a way that we suppose them to have been popular materials of the day. The damask was costly even then, and usually imported from England and other European countries. Some we know came by direct route from India, but home-made turkeywork was often used in its place.

Turkeywork is merely another name for worsted work—generally upon canvas in cross stitch. The name seems to have come from the fact that turkeywork first appears in imitation of turkey rugs used as throws on tables.

Small squares of canvas were worked and then sewn together, and

TURKEYWORK POCKETBOOK ENCLOSING PRIMITIVE VANITY CASE

tufted at the corners. A large needle drew the wool through the mesh in a manner similar to the making of hooked rugs. For chair or stool coverings the whole piece was made in one.

The earliest known mention of samplers is in 1502 in England, and from information given concerning them we may gather that they were copies of Italian handiwork, but somehow we find it difficult to dissociate the sampler from colonial America, for their lettered legends have for us a personal element that makes it difficult for us to associate them with any other period or place.

The earliest samplers in this country were long and narrow. The upper portion was filled with elaborate running designs and below appeared the "tree of life" or an allegorical scene. At the bottom was cut or drawn-work with an occasional alphabet worked in as an integral part of the design, and the whole thing was embroidered in a stitch resembling crewel.

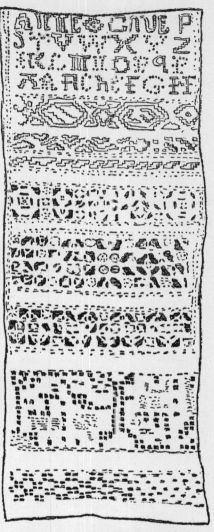

EARLY DRAWNWORK SAMPLER

Only two of the authentic examples of these Seventeenth Century samplers exist, although of the Eighteenth Century we find them in large numbers throughout the colonies, but more particularly in New England, Long Island, New Jersey, and Pennsylvania. The first were English in type but were followed very shortly by a distinctly American style.

Stitching and exquisite embroidery were taught in all finishing schools for girls, and one class of sampler comes from this source. The other class was composed of those made by very young children as a means of learning not only stitching but even the alphabet and figures. Such samplers were often made by girls of but five and six years and were simple and crude compared with those made in the boarding schools.

About 1721 all American samplers displayed Biblical scenes and often legends in Latin. Alphabets were separated from the patterns by rows of cross stitch, Greek fret, or equally simple designs. The running designs showed the "India pink" with vines or the "tree of life." Pennsylvania at this time contributes the Lord's Prayer and Ten Commandments or Creed and the "shepherdess with her flock" pictures. Many of the latter just

escaped being needlework pictures, so large and prominent is the picture part compared with the borders, and so exquisite is the embroidery.

In 1738, Boston comes forward with Adam and Eve, and for many years thereafter this subject remained popular.

By 1750, the heavy religious feeling in this work was lost and we find the pictures taken from nature and daily life. Of this period a beautiful Dorothy Linde sampler remains in the Old South Church of Boston. Both coloring and lettering are unusual and the whole sampler is worked in petit point.

In the cruder examples nature is badly distorted, huge birds light on tiny trees, flowers are larger than sheep, and the gay shepherdess appears three times larger than her house.

NEEDLEWORK PICTURE

By 1760, the sampler again became religious, similar in style to those which had preceded. In 1800, the geneological sampler first appeared. These bore complete family histories, and are delightful.

About 1766, the samplers made in the South nearly all showed the Adam and Eve picture while the same year in Boston witnessed the first serious attempt to reproduce a group of buildings. Prior to this one home had often been shown, but merely as a background for the rest of the picture. But in this year Bath-Sheba Searing produced a whole village on her sampler, and started the widely extended craze for such subject matter.

Although the map sampler was always popular in England it was not

EMBROIDERED BED COVER

until 1775 that Frances Breton created a map of Newport, Rhode Island, the first that we know of in this country. An unknown embroiderer has left us a map of Europe, minutely detailed, and dated 1787.

At this date it becomes possible to identify the various finishing schools by the type of needlework and subject matter that appeared on the samplers created in each, and the great numbers of them in existence warrant a lengthy study of the subject. From this period on little that was new was added to the sampler aside from the eventual, modest clothing of Adam and Eve.

This outline of samplers is without doubt merely a sketch for reference concerning general tendencies at certain periods. Variants appear at every turn that fall under no category mentioned above, but this does not exclude them from their places among worthy American samplers.

Early letters often mention homemade as well as imported laces on the wearing apparel of both men and women. Little is known of its early manufacture except a detailed account written up in an old history of Ipswich, Massachusetts, by one Felt. He describes the making of this lace upon pillows. The pattern drawn upon parchment was attached to the pillow and the entire design outlined with pins stuck upright into the cushion. About them was woven the design. The thread, usually linen, was wound upon bobbins made of chicken bone and uniquely, in America, of bamboo. By 1790, Felt estimates the yearly output of this industry at 41,979 yards.

With the advent of machinery the pillows and bobbins were discarded although the making of lace was still taught to children, as a means of self-support.

At Midway, Massachusetts, the Reverend Horace Dean Walker had a machine of 1,260 shuttles which attracted attention from far and wide. Net was manufactured here and sent with patterns into neighboring homes to be embroidered. Sometimes the designs were made by the embroiderer, and are usually painstaking in detail.

Lace-making was taught in the Moravian School at Bethlehem, Pennsylvania, and in Miss Pierce's Female Academy at Litchfield, Connecticut, and many of the girls in these schools carried their work so far as to make exquisite dresses and wedding veils.

It is impossible to go into a lengthy outline of lace-making, but suffice it to say that after 1800 every current magazine picked up the fad. Darned laces upon net appeared in two popular designs "the cat's eye" and "two and thripenny," from the Ipswich manufactory, and later came an embroidered and linen tape lace.

THE END

GLOSSARY

CONSTRUCTION DETAILS

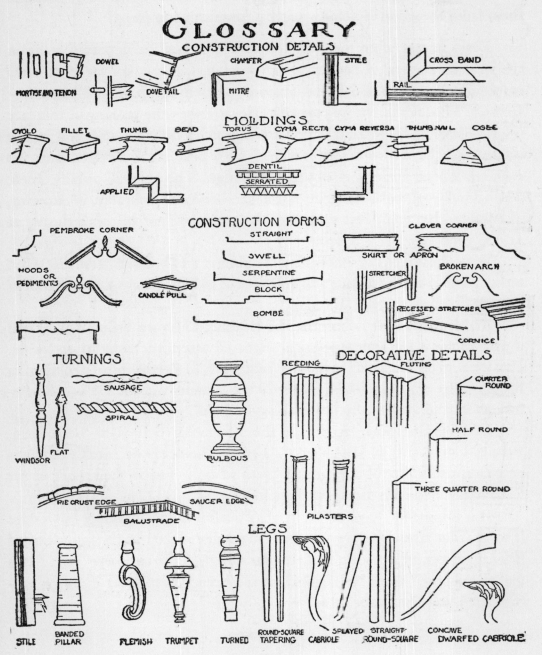

MORTISE AND TENON — DOWEL — DOVETAIL — CHAMFER — MITRE — STILE — RAIL — CROSS BAND

MOLDINGS

OVOLO — FILLET — THUMB — BEAD — TORUS — CYMA RECTA — CYMA REVERSA — THUMB NAIL — OGEE

APPLIED — DENTIL — SERRATED

CONSTRUCTION FORMS

PEMBROKE CORNER — STRAIGHT — SWELL — SERPENTINE — BLOCK — BOMBÉ

HOODS OR PEDIMENTS — CANDLE PULL

CLOVER CORNER — SKIRT OR APRON — BROKEN ARCH — STRETCHER — RECESSED STRETCHER — CORNICE

TURNINGS

SAUSAGE — SPIRAL — BULBOUS

WINDSOR — FLAT

DECORATIVE DETAILS

REEDING — FLUTING — QUARTER ROUND — HALF ROUND — THREE QUARTER ROUND — PILASTERS

PIE CRUST EDGE — SAUCER EDGE — BALUSTRADE

LEGS

STILE — BANDED PILLAR — FLEMISH — TRUMPET — TURNED — ROUND-SQUARE TAPERING — CABRIOLE — SPLAYED ROUND-SQUARE — STRAIGHT — CONCAVE DWARFED CABRIOLE

273

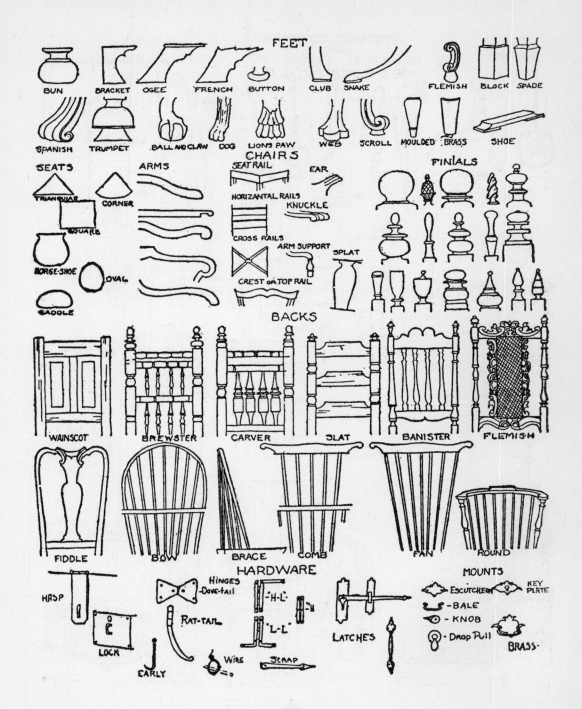

FEET

BUN · BRACKET · OGEE · FRENCH · BUTTON · CLUB · SNAKE · FLEMISH · BLOCK · SPADE

SPANISH · TRUMPET · BALL AND CLAW · DOG · LIONS PAW · WEB · SCROLL · MOULDED · BRASS · SHOE

CHAIRS

SEATS

TRIANGULAR · CORNER · SQUARE · HORSE-SHOE · OVAL · SADDLE

ARMS

SEAT RAIL · EAR · HORIZANTAL RAILS · KNUCKLE · CROSS RAILS · ARM SUPPORT · SPLAT · CREST or TOP RAIL

FINIALS

BACKS

WAINSCOT · BREWSTER · CARVER · SLAT · BANISTER · FLEMISH

FIDDLE · BOW · BRACE · COMB · FAN · ROUND

HARDWARE

HASP · LOCK · EARLY · Hinges-Dove-tail · Rat-tail · Wire · Scrap · H-L · L-L · LATCHES

MOUNTS

Escutcheon · KEY PLATE · -BALE · -KNOB · Drop Pull · BRASS·

274

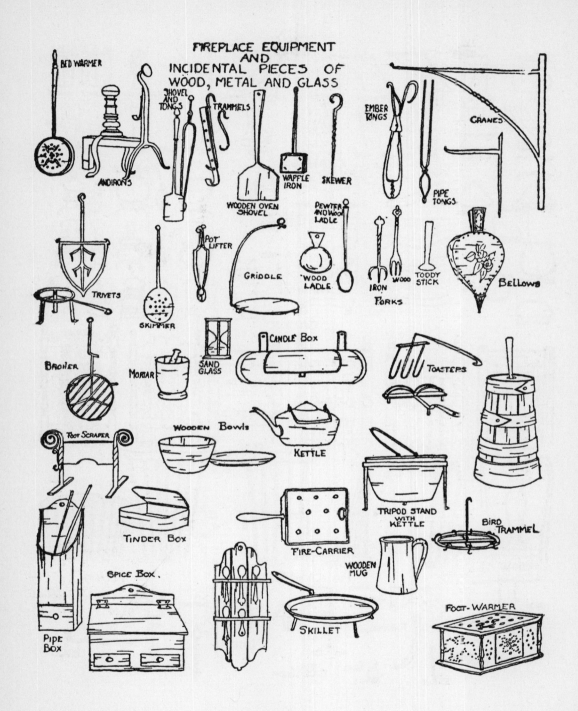

FIREPLACE EQUIPMENT
AND
INCIDENTAL PIECES OF
WOOD, METAL AND GLASS

BED WARMER

SHOVEL AND TONGS

TRAMMELS

ANDIRONS

WOODEN OVEN SHOVEL

WAFFLE IRON

SKEWER

EMBER TONGS

CRANES

PIPE TONGS

TRIVETS

SKIMMER

POT LIFTER

GRIDDLE

PEWTER AND WOOD LADLE

WOOD LADLE

IRON

WOOD

FORKS

TODDY STICK

BELLOWS

BROILER

MORTAR

SAND GLASS

CANDLE BOX

TOASTERS

WOODEN BOWLS

KETTLE

FOOT SCRAPER

TINDER BOX

FIRE-CARRIER

TRIPOD STAND WITH KETTLE

BIRD TRAMMEL

PIPE BOX

SPICE BOX.

WOODEN MUG

SKILLET

FOOT-WARMER

BRASSES
1640–1800

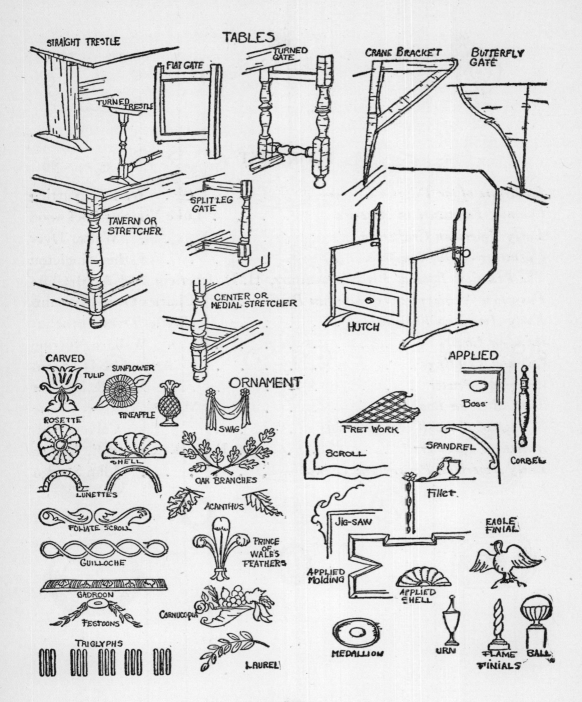

TABLES

STRAIGHT TRESTLE

TURNED TRESTLE

FLAT GATE

TURNED GATE

CRANE BRACKET

BUTTERFLY GATE

TAVERN OR STRETCHER

SPLIT LEG GATE

CENTER OR MEDIAL STRETCHER

HUTCH

CARVED

TULIP

SUNFLOWER

ROSETTE

PINEAPPLE

SHELL

SWAG

ORNAMENT

OAK BRANCHES

LUNETTES

ACANTHUS

FOLIATE SCROLL

GUILLOCHE

PRINCE OF WALES FEATHERS

GADROON

FESTOONS

CARNUCOPIA

TRIGLYPHS

LAUREL

APPLIED

BOSS

FRET WORK

SCROLL

SPANDREL

CORBEL

FILLET

JIG-SAW

APPLIED MOLDING

APPLIED SHELL

EAGLE FINIAL

MEDALLION

URN

FLAME FINIALS

BALL

277

BOOK LIST

Furniture of the Pilgrim Century . . . . Wallace Nutting
Colonial Furniture in America . . . . . . Luke Vincent Lockwood
Early American Craftsmen . . . . Walter Dyer
Furniture of Our Forefathers . . . . Esther Singleton
The Practical Book of Period Furniture, H. D. Eberlein and A. McClure
Furniture Masterpieces of Duncan Phyfe . . Charles Over Cornelius
Early American Furniture . . . . . . Charles Over Cornelius
Windsor Chairs . . . . Wallace Nutting
Colonial Lighting . . . . Arthur H. Hayward
American Pewter . . . . J. B. Kerfoot
The Old Clock Book . . . . Mrs. N. Hudson Moore
A Book of Hand-Woven Coverlets . . . . . Eliza Calvert Hall
American Samplers . . . . E. S. Bolton and E. J. Cole
Early American Pottery and China . . . . John Spargo

INDEX

INDEX